Against Modern
Humanism

Against Modern Humanism

On The Culture of Ego

Jeff Bergner

Rambling Ridge Press

Rambling Ridge Press, LLC
4430 East Beach Drive
Norfolk, Virginia 23518

Bergner, Jeffrey T.
    Against modern humanism : on the culture of ego /
Jeff Bergner.
    p. cm.
    LCCN 2013906212
    ISBN 978-0-9890402-0-4 Hardcover
    ISBN 978-0-9890402-1-1 Softcover
1. Humanism. 2. Ego (Psychology) 3. Idealism,
German.   I. Title.
B821.B47 2013   144
                    QBI13-600063

Printed in the United States of America.

[Nature] has called us into life, into the whole universe, there to be spectators to her games and eager competitors; and she therefore from the first breathed into our hearts an unconquerable passion for whatever is great and more divine than ourselves.

Longinus,
On the Sublime

CONTENTS

INTRODUCTION

INTRODUCTION

How shall we live a good life? Is this even a serious question? Is there only one way to live a good life, or are there many, each to be decided as we please? Why should we suppose that one way of life is better, or more fully human, than any other? For that matter, how would we measure what is to count as "better?"

The dominant contemporary understanding of how to live a good life is perfectly captured in a popular advertising slogan: a human being should "be all you can be." This slogan might seem unobjectionable, even trite. Who could disagree that, whatever else, we should be all that we can be? But how are we to be all we can be? Perhaps the slogan is empty, a simple restatement of the question of how best to live.

This slogan is not as innocent or as empty as it seems. It seems to point everywhere and nowhere—but this itself is a very specific kind of answer to the question of the best human life. We might call this answer modern secular humanism, and if the slogan seems innocent and unobjectionable it is less because it is self-evident than because it dominates so fully the intellectual and cultural life of modernity.

In today's dominant view, we human beings are not assigned fixed stations or places in the universe. Nor are we controlled or driven by powers outside ourselves, be they called gods or anything else. We are the masters of our own fate—or at least we can be if we choose to be. We can change ourselves and the world. We have choices and we can be otherwise than we are. We can employ our reason in the service of our choices. We have it within our power to become virtually whatever we want. We can invent and re-invent ourselves, almost at will. It makes little difference where we were born—we can become citizens of the wider world. Our social or economic class of origin makes little difference—we can become fabulously successful. Nor are we much constrained by weight, hair color, unattractive body parts or even age—we can shape and reshape ourselves with the products of modern medicine and cosmetics. It scarcely matters if we are hopeless debtors or inveterate sinners—we can be absolved, born again, and begin over. And over and over. We strive mightily against each and every limit, real or perceived, on the boundless freedom to be all we can be.

In the view of modern humanism, we humans are the measure of all things. We do not judge our purposes in terms of what is larger than ourselves; the larger world is to be employed to serve our purposes. Our task is to overcome false and seeming limitations. We have somewhere "within" ourselves, as we say, the irreducible freedom to become all we can.

The entire modern world is moved by this restless yearning to be free of limits. Those institutions and those regimes which seek today to restrict human freedom must do so by sheer force, because they can no longer rely simply upon the weight of authority or the antiquity of tradition. Even religious fundamentalists—orthodox Jews, literalist Christians and Islamists—struggle against the gravitational attraction of the modern pursuit of radical human freedom.

And who today can doubt the transforming power of the pursuit of human freedom? Who can deny that human science has remade the entire planet? No aspect of the world, from our genes within to the constellations above, escapes the human power to understand and to manipulate. Prohibitions, taboos and ways of life thought for millennia to be "natural" have succumbed to the corrosive power of human freedom.

But before we accept too quickly this human freedom to shape ourselves and the world—to be all we can be—as the deepest, most essential human quality, let us listen for a moment to another voice. Consider the words of the ancient Greek philosopher Heracleitus, who is reputed to have said that "character for man is destiny."[*] What does this mean? Like any good ancient Greek, Heracleitus thought that a man is truly revealed in how he conducts his life, not in a mysterious internal power to do otherwise than he has done. A man's character is revealed as the challenges of his life unfold; and a man's life unfolds toward that destiny to which his character impels him.

The very concept of "destiny" rings strangely on modern ears. When we watch a Greek tragedy whose protagonist is led ineluctably to the actions he takes—and these actions condemn him to the foreordained outcome—we moderns revolt. We look for ways that this outcome need not have occurred, for ways the protagonist might have chosen differently, and for ways to ensure this does not happen again. But of course this is to miss the point of tragedy: we cannot escape the destiny to which our character impels us. Indeed, so completely does the ineluctable force of destiny contradict our striving to choose and to be free of limits, we moderns do not even *wish* to understand it.

So, too, with destiny's equally unforgiving partner "tragedy." A genuine tragedy works inescapably toward the terrible conclusion of destiny. We moderns do not understand the meaning of tragedy this way. We might hear, for example, about the death of a teenage driver in a one car speeding accident. We say that the death of this young person is "tragic."

---

[*]Heracleitus, *Ancilla to the Pre-Socratic Philosophers*, fragment #119. See also Epicharmes, #17 and Democritus, # 6

But what is meant? We most assuredly do not mean that his character was his destiny, that the rashness and excess which his character displayed condemned him to this death. We mean instead that his death is sad, or at best untimely. We thus dilute the meaning of tragedy; tragedy becomes synonymous with any sad or unhappy event. And we look for ways to structure our lives and our social institutions to make such an outcome less likely for others.

The Modern Ego

The idea that character is destiny is far indeed from the way we moderns understand ourselves. For modern secular humanism, who we are intrinsically or essentially is decidedly *not* the totality of our conduct, much less our station in life, our destiny, or a character which defines us. To the contrary, who or what we really are is thought to lie somehow "behind" our conduct; it is hidden within us and transcends the many choices of our lives. We choose one way, but we could always have chosen differently. It is the power to choose and the agent of this choosing which modern humanism identifies with what it means to be human.

But who—or what—is the agent of human choosing? Who or what is this being who benefits from the power to understand and to transform the world? This being is usually called the "I" or the "ego." This is the name of the being that lies at the root of, or prior to, all human choice and action. This is the being within us that manifests the freedom to choose. Ego is at once the agent and the beneficiary of the capability to change the world and ourselves, including our ability to procreate, our moods, our memories and even our intellectual capacities. Its existence seems validated by countless daily confirmations of the human ability to transform the world and ourselves.

But who or what *is* this powerful but elusive ego? Who or

what is this agent of human freedom which enables we humans to be all we can be? No one has ever seen an ego, of course; ego's existence can only be inferred from the choices and actions from which it is presumed that these choices and actions in turn derive. We seem unable to learn anything definite about ego by observing the lives of actual people, since human choices and actions manifest themselves in so many different ways. As the Buddha long ago observed in the *Digha Nikaya*, ego cannot be "witnessed at all, and those who believe in it are likened to a man who says that he is in love with the most beautiful woman in the land, but is unable to specify her name, her family, or her appearance."

We might ask why modern humanism finds it necessary, or even useful, to suppose that this "X," this ego, lies behind our choices at all. Why not simply do away with this supposition altogether and, as scientific materialism purports to do, study the laws of motion or the patterns of human behavior? Why don't we dissolve this "ego superstition" into matter in motion? Why don't we join modern scientists and their philosophical popularizers who make precisely this assertion: there is only matter in motion. But the idea that matter in motion is what there is, is of course itself an idea. If this were not enough to display the startling superficiality of this claim, modern materialists then demand that everyone acknowledge the truth of their assertion—as if it is critically important how people choose to *think* about the world.

This raises a deeper question. In the modern world two major strains of thought co-exist side by side: the determinism of modern science and the many voluntarist philosophies of pragmatism, existentialism, self-transformation and even nihilism which dominate our culture. How can these views co-exist with one another? Why do human freedom and the culture of self-improvement and self-transformation become salient at precisely the same period as modern science? This question has been asked in a pointed way in John Paul II's encyclical letter "Fides et Ratio." How, and why, do existential philosophies of freedom in their many forms serve as the historical companions of mature modern science? Upon what deeper basis can the seemingly incompatible viewpoints of freely choosing egos and scientific determinism co-exist with one another?

The answer may well surprise: modern humanism received its deepest and most influential impulse from the philosophy of German idealism. This may be surprising because so many advocates of contemporary humanism—existentialists, pragmatists, social scientists, psychologists, philosophers of science, and purveyors of the popular culture of self-improvement—are generally unaware of the intellectual origins of their own views. Indeed, many of these schools of thought, to the extent they are self-reflective at all, understand themselves to stand in opposition to the German idealist philosophy upon which they rest. While they may have rejected the historicism and system-building of German idealist philosophy, they have accepted uncritically the deeper egoism which lies at its heart.

It is the aim of this essay to demonstrate how this is so, and how it is possible that there is no contradiction between a culture of scientific determinism and a culture of self-transforming egos. We will address this question more fully in Chapter Five. For now, we can summarize. Why don't we moderns dissolve the "ego superstition" into matter in motion? Who is the "we" who is supposed to carry out such a dissolution? Is it not we egos whose interests and intents are the determiners of which patterns and regularities we do and do not find useful—and therefore of what our modern science will consist? Doesn't this thought guide our philosophy of science, which roots our scientific paradigms in human interests? And our social sciences, which root our research into economic, political and social patterns in the service of human desires? And our pragmatic and existential philosophies, which root our every thought and action in human intent? And our modern humanist psychology, which roots its investigations in the service of what will free the human ego from its external determinants? And our contemporary analytic philosophy, which sets as a chief task to understand the domain of human intentionality?

German idealist philosophy explains the theoretical basis of modern science—and thus defends it—by rooting it in the freedom of ego. It seeks to reconcile freedom and necessity, human freedom and scientific determinism—but it does so by placing theory fully into the service of human practice. Early modern philosophy had severed the connections which existed between bodies and minds in historic church Christianity, and for that matter in most common sense understandings as well. The human essence was completely and thoroughly de-physicalized. The human body, including the brain, was no more or less than any other being in the external world of extension. It thus became permissible to manipulate and alter the human body, since the body is merely the physical vessel which exists side by side with mind, the true human essence. In penetrating to the laws or patterns which describe the processes of the external world—and those laws or patterns are of course themselves ideas—mind learns how to manipulate the external world in new and impressive ways. But the cost of this was a deepening estrangement between the human mind and the rest of the world.

It was just this problem of mind/ body dualism which German idealist philosophy of the late eighteenth and early nineteenth centuries set out to resolve. The "mind" of early modern philosophers was first dissolved into a series of rules by Immanuel Kant. Kant argued that reason could not penetrate to the intrinsic being of anything. The world in which things exist "for their own sakes," if it exists at all, is impenetrable to us. Reason can know, but it can know only that which its own processes or rules of thinking make possible to know. Reason can know not because of a privileged connection to the world "out there," but because it can know a world of its own thinking.

It was not long before Kant's successors understood the possible implications of this view. If reason could not discover anything about the world in and of itself, what world was reason learning about? What was this world spun out by the processes and rules of human reason, which in turn reason then laid claim to grasp? The answer was readily at hand: reason is powerful, but only because what it understands is a world which is somehow of our own making. It is not powerful because it can attain to knowledge of a pre-existing world which is other to us; there is no "other to us" about which we can have any knowledge. Indeed, what is "other to us" is a world which is itself our own idea. What there is to know is the world or worlds which we create. Post-Kantian German idealist philosophy located the essence of what it means to be human in the destructive/ constructive act of creation, in the power to create a world or worlds which we then can know.

Why This Matters

Why does any of this matter? What difference does it make how we understand who or what we are as human beings? The American philosopher Chauncey Wright, for example, wrote in a letter to a friend that "to stake any serious human concern on the truth of this or that philosophical theory seems to me... in the highest degree arrogant or absurd." Philosophers have been ridiculed from time immemorial for their irrelevance to practical life; they have been portrayed falling into holes while looking up at the stars, or exiting rooms only through doors after denying the reality of walls. Empty speculation may indeed offer little guidance as to how to live. But from that conclusion it is only a short step to conventional wisdom, everyday understandings and "common sense" as the proper standards to which to repair. But why these standards, which are often obviously wrong or limited or transient, should guide human life is no easier to say.

What difference does it make how we think about who or what we are? What difference does it make how we understand ourselves and our purpose (s)? One who thinks of oneself as a servant of a god named Allah, commanded to die in a glorious and holy act of destruction, can fly an aircraft into the World Trade Center at 400 miles an hour. Such an action is not possible, and barely even comprehensible, to a person who thinks of himself or herself as a businessman in a commercial republic or as a suburban soccer mom. One who thinks of himself as a member of a tribe (or a family, or gang, or nation) whose perpetuation is prized above all else can act with honor and lay down one's life for that end. One who believes one is everlasting soul briefly trapped in a physical body, can act with little concern about preserving that body. And one who believes one's entire psychosomatic being is at risk of permanent bliss or torment will take seriously indeed the path to salvation.

Do these self-understandings *cause* these respective ways of life or do they merely accompany them, even rationalize them? Are they, as a Marxist might say, epiphenomena? Perhaps our self-understandings are causal; perhaps they are not. Perhaps our self-understandings and our actions are both determined together. Whatever else, self-understandings and ways of life seem indisputably bound together. Perhaps further scientific research will discover that all manner of self-understandings can be put into peoples' minds by chemical or genetic manipulation. This could prove to be a very economical way to alter how human beings think about themselves compared with the more laborious ways such as preaching, instruction and questioning which have been employed to date. But for all of that, this convenience would not diminish one iota the force of the fundamental question: how *should* we rightly think of ourselves and others?

The Greek slave Epictetus raised this question in his *Discourses* (Book II, 10) when he asked "How is it possible to discover a man's duties from the designations which he bears?" In the history of Western thought, this is not a strange or unusual question. Each of the major Western understandings— up until modern humanism—points to preferred way(s) of life. Each does so because it roots the meaning of human being in an essential quality from which the preferred way of life is derived or, better said, already more or less implied.

All of the Torah, for example, is an answer to the question of how to live. Here one finds an implicit metaphysics which is radically different than ours today. This radically different understanding is often obscured by contemporary interpret-tations, which read back into the Torah many of today's assumptions and prejudices. The duties and obligations in the books of Moses follow directly from the description of the member of the tribe which worships Yahweh. It is through the rules which are given by Yahweh that one finds the realization of what it means to be a human being and how to live accordingly.

So, too, with the ancient Greek idea of "soul," whose purpose or function was to explain the differing kinds of being which comprise the world. "Soul" is the animating force of life. As such, it poses questions which were not at the center of the Torah. Where does soul "come from" and where does it "go" at death? The ancient Greek understanding of human being as a special kind of ensouled being points to a life which tends soul, a care which is most eloquently presented above all by Plato's Socrates.

Historic church Christianity fused together aspects of Jewish teaching and Greek philosophy into a new view of what it means to be a human being. It did so in a very surprising and long-lasting way. The creation of historic church Christianity was the psychosomatic unity of the human being which enjoys (or suffers) everlasting continuity, even after death. The Christian conception of perpetually embodied will points to a decision of faith in which the will is either turned toward or turned away from God, and thus saves or condemns the entire psychosomatic being forever. As such, it raised the question of the best way to live to epic proportions.

Early modern thought turned sharply from church Christianity to locate what is human exclusively in the mind. While practicing Christians today tend to see their doctrine as a spiritual antidote to the material excesses of modern life, the early modern philosophical revolt against Christianity was, to the contrary, a thoroughgoing idealism which repudiated the physicality of Christian doctrine. Even the de-physicalized human being of early modern thought seems to point to a preferred way of life—a way in which mind penetrates to the rules or patterns of the extended universe's motion in order to know being as it really acts, thus better to fulfill the human essence as mind.

Each of these broad understandings describes carefully the essence of what it means to be human. Each aims for the virtue which Confucius called "the rectification of names." When things are rightly named, and thus rightly understood, they will be rightly used. Each aims to promote the kind of life most appropriate to human being. When humans are rightly named, and thus properly understood, their duties will follow and right action will result.

The modern understanding of human being as ego, however, is radically different. In subordinating mind to ego, no meaningful "ought" can be discovered. The entire world is opened out as the *creation* of ego, and such a world can offer no context through which to offer guidance for the choices of that ego. From this many consequences can be drawn. One consequence is of course nihilism. Another is sadness and alienated subjectivity. Another is the existential choice to live courageously in a world where human ego can find no anchor, because *we* have created the storm on which we are tossed about.

The modern ego, which transcends all limitations which fix it in space, time and its own history, is empty. It is rootless, boundless striving, directionless and devoid of content. It is the pure power to choose. Ego is free to choose—but who can say what, or why, it should choose? Moral guidance depends upon an understanding of choices that are worthy in light of the essence, or the nature, of the chooser. But if there is no human essence or nature except the pure power to choose, what guidance could possibly be obtained from any source outside the ego? What source external to ego could stand above it and offer such guidance?

How we understand ourselves thus is consequential for how we as individuals live. But it also creates momentous consequences for the aims and structures of our social and political institutions. To illustrate, we might note that the American government created at the end of the 18th century was a product of early modern philosophy. It is said to value freedom highly, and indeed it does. But why? This government was not designed to satisfy directly the desires of egos but to secure and preserve the conditions for the free exercise of mind. The freedom guaranteed by the American government was intended to provide a context within which individuals could choose their own, higher ends. What are these ends? The new American government reflected fully the early modern idea of mind as the human essence: the goal was to allow mind to be free. This might mean free to worship one's god; it might mean free to seek knowledge of the universe without any reference to god at all; or it might mean the application of mind to the worlds of nature or commerce. What is required in all cases, however, is freedom of inquiry and expression, which in turn requires toleration. When the free exercise of mind is understood as the essence of human being, toleration is the cardinal virtue.

The structure of American constitutional government is intended as a creation of mind which reflects what is most essential about being human. Its authors understood it as the result of scientific inquiry into human nature, and its precise form as an "experiment" which, like all science, is always subject to revision. On this view, there is a sense of prudence about what government will and will not be asked to do. It will not be asked to do any and all things human egos might desire, but it will be expected to maintain the conditions for the free exercise of the human mind. There is a corresponding willingness to rely on external devices to foster this central task of government. What helps to do this—what helps to moderate the demands which ego might make of government—is to be esteemed. This might well include revealed religion. Not all revealed religions necessarily moderate the ends of govern-ment, but those that do are to be respected. George Washington speaks of the necessity of religious belief to maintain a sound political order; in his Farewell Address of 1796, he calls religion and morality the "finest props of men and citizens." Washington does not here address the truth of religious claims, but their utility; he admits the possibility that "minds of peculiar structure" might not require religious belief to lead moral lives. But as to the importance of certain kinds of religious belief to support the popular virtues of moderation and toleration he is unambiguous. A belief that humans are essentially mind –whose task is to come to knowledge of and conformity with the rules of the universe and of our own natures—will foster a government which makes the free expression of mind its chief aim and toleration of free inquiry its chief tool. It will avail itself of auxiliary tools like religion and morality, as needed, to help support the instrumental virtue of freedom.

It is much different for a government understood to operate in a world comprised of human egos. In such a world the political order, like every human institution, becomes an instrument for the direct satisfaction of ego. No longer is there a sense of prudence about what government should and should not be asked to do; whatever government can do to satisfy the desires of ego is fully appropriate. As the creation of ego, rather than as an instrumental creation of mind to preserve freedom, government can and should aim to do whatever ego seeks. Government policies are the result of competition among egos, and government policies will thus reflect the choices of the more numerous or the more powerful. Accordingly, the politics of today point everywhere and nowhere. It is not that today's competition of egos points unfailingly to tyranny, though it often does; it points to whatever ego pleases. Beneath the emotive rhetoric of today's political sloganeering—"fairness" and the like—there is no fixed understanding of the purpose of government at all. In his commentary on Goethe's *Faust*, the philosopher George Santayana captures the essence of the modern government official: "his ultimate satisfaction in his work is not founded on any good done, but on a passionate willfulness. He calls the thing he wants for others good, because he wants to bestow it on them, not because they naturally want it for themselves." This willfulness is the hallmark of contemporary politics.

And because the free exercise of ego creates the very purpose of government, how could artificial bounds or external supports like religion be useful? Religious claims often argue for bounds or limits on the free expression of political choices. As such religion today is not a "prop," but a *problem* for smoothly functioning government. Religious belief today is not understood as a protector of good government, but as an obstacle to it. All that remains of civic virtue is the hope that a nation of freely choosing egos will somehow miraculously choose to moderate or subordinate their desires to produce political harmony. This, however, is an outcome little to be expected. A government of, by and for freely choosing egos will soon enough be a government which operates by command rather than consensus. A world of freely choosing egos is not a world of happily interdependent and naturally reinforcing beings. It is a world in which moral life gives way to moralism, values to value "clarification," ethos to ethicists, and persisting substance to pointless process.

Understanding ourselves as ego has another significant consequence. This self-understanding seems to lack the force or the power that older, more narrowly essentialist views of human beings offer. When egos come hard up against challenges from more coherent and focused views of the ends of man, they seem to wither; they cannot find a basis on which to meet these challenges. For all of the assertiveness of modern egos, they seem to lack a firm context which offers support for their desires. They seem to have no grounds on which to defend themselves or upon which sacrifice would make sense. Who, for example, most vigorously defends the modern West when it comes under attack from fundamentalist Islam, a theology diametrically opposed to a world of freely choosing egos? Is it the outspoken advocates of modernity, who argue against any and all moral codes or any revealed religious truth? Is it the libertines, or the apostles of liberation from all social, sexual or theological restrictions on the free exercise of human ego? It seems not. Rather, it turns out that the modern West's strongest protectors are believing Christians, defenders of Israel, and men and women of honor who are moved, at least in part, by other and older understandings of what it means to be human.

On the Restoration of Human Finitude

We have traversed a long path to reach our world today, a world in which ego reigns supreme. And as one might suppose with any dominant form of thinking, there are satisfactions to be drawn from today's world of ego. Indeed, there is much to be prized in the contemporary secular view of human being. It breaks down ideas that have too narrowly fixed the essence of being human. It opens us to expansive possibilities, and beyond the temptation to fasten too hastily upon one or another human quality as the essence of the human way of being. This, and the corrosive skepticism that accompanies it, surely has its positive uses.

But at the same time, the radical openness of the contemporary world of ego seems always somehow at odds with how human life is actually and truly lived. We never seem to be quite as free in practice as the philosophy of ego would suggest. Our philosophy and self-understanding suppose we are powerful and great in the scheme of things, but we learn in hard times that we are not. We cannot live without making choices all the time, but we seem at bottom unable to find contentment with the choices we have made. We somehow know that we are not free at every given moment, and that if we were, it would come at the cost of obliterating rather than expanding the world that lies before us.

We have come to an impasse: we are the masters of our world, but only because the world is one which we create. German idealism freed reason from its enslavement to our passions and to the more or less fixed set of norms supposedly given to us in the form of "moral sentiments"—only to enslave reason to a new and more imperious master, the creative ego. With no possibility of knowing anything about a world which is "given" to us, ego sets out to create worlds of its own. Our passions are no more or less given to ego than is a free-standing external world which exists in and for itself; they too are subject to the destructive/ creative power of ego. Reason can know what it regards as truth, but it is invariably the truth which ego seeks. And reason can know about morality, but morality is invariably the freedom of ego. In an arresting phrase, William Wordsworth said that human reason is not a mere pensioner on external forms. For German idealism, reason and morality are both mere pensioners on the world of ego.

This is the problem we face today. Is it possible for us to move beyond the circular impasse which is our world of ego? Is it possible to know anything about a world outside of us? Is it possible to re-gain a sense of human finitude by a way of knowing that is not fully in the service of ego? We might put this question another way: is it possible to live in a world in which human beings know their finitude without relying on the commands of revealed religion? Nietzsche asked the question: if there are gods, how could he stand not to be god? We might ask a different question: if there are no gods, how can we live without the illusion that we are gods?

This leads us back to the underlying question: who or what

are we human beings? Kant is famous for asking three pointed questions of humanity: What can we know? What ought we do? And what may we hope? In a cryptic formulation in the *Jaesche Logik* (9:25) he rightly said that these questions are all contained within another: Who or what are we human beings?

If we are to understand our world today—and more importantly how we humans truly are—we must step out of the assumptions of the philosophy of ego. Is this possible? Perhaps it is not widely to be expected. But it is possible, for the understanding of human beings as ego is after all simply a model. It is in this way no different than Plato's charioteer, or Hume's amalgam of passions, moral sentiments and reason, or Freud's id, ego and superego—it is a way to think about who we are. Modern egoism arose from an attempt to solve a specific set of philosophical problems, and it has persisted because it offers a set of satisfactions to those who hold it. But if we understand it fully—and therefore its limitations—we can move beyond it and escape the impasse in which it leaves us, as well as the self-indulgent view of our unlimited power.

In doing so, we must keep open the very difficult and problematical question of how, and in what ways, the world is "given" to us and how, and in what ways, it is created by us. We cannot close off thought about this. We humans of course play some role in creating our own world, not merely our social world but the world of "nature" as well. As Heidegger might say, nothing in the world would be revealed as it is without us. We seem to be required to help to give being to beings. There is an indisputable human role in the creation of our world, and in this sense no philosophy on earth is shallower than dogmatic materialism. But to conclude from this that human egos are therefore creating this world out of the whole cloth of our human interests and intents—with no participation from anything or anyone outside our ego—is altogether without warrant. We will conclude with the judgment that modern egoism vastly overstates its case. We will conclude that its premise that no part of the world is "given" to us—and might also therefore be uncovered by human reason—is without justification. The conclusion of modern egoism is precisely the opposite mistake which earlier traditions made in closing off this question too quickly and in making dogmatic claims about our essential nature. We will argue that a measure of openness and humility about the "givenness" or lack of "givenness" of the world far better suits us.

We will conclude with some modest suggestions about how human life is best and most fully lived. Even though modest, such suggestions might strike today's readers as arrogant, if not quixotic. The arrogance is easy to understand: it arises from trying to say anything at all about how to be truly and fully human. It is arrogant because doing so requires overturning the dominant contemporary model of human beings and restoring reason to a role in which it can be directive, because it can know something outside itself in a real way, and not simply how to satisfy the desires of ego.

The modesty is perhaps less obvious. The suggestions here are modest because they do not dictate a complete menu of principles and rules to guide each and every choice or action of our daily life, as might a revealed religion. These suggestions offer only a general orientation toward life and the world. This is consistent with both the power and the limits of human reason. We will say more of this orientation at the conclusion of this essay. For now, we will say simply that it is an orientation of gratitude. It is the hallmark of contemporary egoism to suppose that the world is one in which nothing is *given* to human ego, but a world in which, as our creation, we possess an indisputable right to everything. A sense of gratitude is predictably rare in this kind of world.

ONE

ETHOS:

ON BELONGING TO A TRIBE

. . . each according to its kind

Genesis 1:24

ETHOS:

ON BELONGING TO A TRIBE

Interpreting an ancient text is akin to an archeological investigation. The words lie before us, but they are overlaid by layers of tradition through which we now read them. In the case of the five books of Moses, the first layer of interpretation comes from the evolution of Judaism itself. For although the Torah remains the central point of the Jewish faith, it has been elaborated and developed through centuries of textual exegesis. Some of this exegesis arguably takes us closer to the original intent of the text; but more often it responds to questions and concerns that arose later and from other schools of thought. As in the case of Christian doctrine, for example, the Greek concept of soul became a major concern of second temple and subsequent Judaism. And just as did Christianity and Islam, Judaism developed a mystical strand. In Kabbalah, Jewish mystics aimed to recast and downplay the many anthropo-morphic descriptions of Yahweh in the books of Moses, seeing them as emanations of a more abstract, more sublime, and less accessible creator.

Christianity deposited a second layer of interpretation on the books of Moses. The idea that the Hebrew Bible is an "old" testament which is supplemented and completed by a later "new" testament has produced understandings that seem distant from anything that could have been in the minds of the authors of the books of Moses. Like Talmudic exegesis, these later elaborations are often clever and invariably interesting; but they are not more reliable interpretations of the original text.[*]

A third layer of interpretation derives from the Enlightenment tradition of individualism. In its most pointed form, eighteenth century Enlightenment criticism regarded the demands of tribal life expressed in the Hebrew Bible and other ancient texts as a "trick" whereby self-interested priestly elites manipulated the people. In the nineteenth century, Karl Marx offered a variant of this view in arguing that elites were not self-consciously tricking the people, but that both elites and masses expressed the consciousness appropriate to their system of production. As such, both elites and masses operated within a restricted horizon of understanding (though elites did benefit at the expense of the masses), the transcendence of which Marx supposed would at last arrive with the dissolution of modern capitalism.

Today's prevalent interpretations of the Torah constitute a fourth layer which stands between us and the words of the books of Moses. By and large, today's interpretations are a response to contemporary universalist criticism of the books of Moses. They aim to reconcile the jarring words of the Torah with today's standards of what is reasonable, universal, and humane. For example, a typical gloss on the words "an eye for an eye" aims invariably to dilute and explain away the injunction. It is argued that "an eye for an eye" does not mean quite what it plainly seems to say, that it was scarcely ever followed in practice, and that in any event what purpose it might once have had is no longer relevant today.

It is surely commendable—up to a point—to draw out of ancient texts meanings that can be reconciled with the

---

[*] Sigmund Freud says in *Moses and Monotheism*: "it is not attractive to be classed with the Scholastics and Talmudists who are satisfied to exercise their ingenuity, unconcerned how far removed their conclusions may be from the truth."

prevalent beliefs of the contemporary world. But in doing this, current sensibilities are set up as the arbiter, and we often learn more about today's values than about the texts themselves. Here we side with Spinoza against Maimonides: one's faith may be a loose combination of rational individualism and the teachings of the Torah, but one should not confuse that faith with what Moses was trying to teach. Artfully contrived but wholly implausible efforts to make Moses "relevant" miss the unique force and power of the Mosaic teachings. If the books of Moses have lessons to teach, it is not because they confirm each of our current prejudices; it is because they do not.

If we strip away the layers of interpretation that have accumulated over the centuries, what do we find in the teachings of the books of Moses? In the first place, we find just that: teachings. They are the teachings of what it means to live in a tribe, a tribe through which one finds the full measure of one's humanity. It is not necessary to exhort normal human beings to eat and to drink, to enjoy sex, or to seek a measure of security and economic predictability in their lives. One supposes for this reason that the teachings and exhortations of the book of Moses are useful – perhaps even required – because of centrifugal tendencies away from tribal life. For example, the command to put no other gods before Yahweh implies the temptation to do just that, and the books of Moses are replete with stories in which the people of Israel did just that.

The teachings of the books of Moses do not therefore provide a full account of the Hebrew people. That story is immeasurably richer and more complex than the commands of Yahweh expressed in the books of Moses, partially consisting of struggles against these very teachings. Nevertheless, these teachings represent the doctrines and the commands which express what it means to live in the tribe of Israel. The books of Moses present a world of sharp and permanent distinctions between kinds of beings; a world in which each being finds its meaning as an instance of a kind, or a type; and a world in which humans realize their essence in and through the tribe of which they are a member.

To Be Set Apart

It is a source of curiosity why the book of Leviticus should stand in the middle of the five books of Moses. Why should this legalistic document, with its myriad prohibitions and rituals, stand right in the center – and indeed interrupt – the long journey from the creation through the Egyptian captivity to the forty years of wandering up to the edge of the promised land? What is its purpose and its role in this otherwise history-ical narrative? In his magisterial translation and commentary on the books of Moses, Robert Alter stresses the importance of the word "*hivdil*" in Leviticus. *Hivdil* means to divide, to differentiate, to set apart. What is divided or set apart is the source of the rituals and prohibitions of Leviticus.

But the importance of *hivdil* goes far beyond the doctrines of Leviticus; *hivdil* stands at the very core of each and every one of the five books of Moses. It is by virtue of the rites and practices set out in Leviticus that the people of Israel express their unique relationship with Yahweh. It is this relationship with Yahweh which sets apart the tribe of Israel from all other people. *Hivdil*, or setting apart, begins in the first chapter of Genesis and continues through the last chapter of Deuteronomy.

Hivdil reflects the sharp and permanent distinctions between the kinds of beings which exist, Yahweh included. Each kind of being is what it is by virtue of being separated from, or set apart from, other kinds of beings which exist. These distinctions are not happenstance, or casual, or temporary. They are certainly not human conventions. They are established by Yahweh and as such are to be understood and defended. It is not too much to say that *hivdil* is the metaphysical basis upon which Mosaic monotheism rests – though of course the books of Moses make just the reverse claim.

The single most important distinction, or differentiation, in the books of Moses is the distinction between Yahweh and all other kinds of being, including gods and men. Yahweh stands alone and unique among all kinds of being. In fairness, there is a certain ambiguity in the books of Moses about the status of other gods. In some passages, the gods of other nations seem to enjoy the status of lesser gods, that is, somewhat intermediate between Yahweh and human beings. They possess powers which, while far inferior to those of Yahweh, seem nevertheless to qualify them as gods. In other passages, the distinction is drawn more sharply, suggesting that the gods of other peoples are no gods at all, but merely imaginary beings who are (wrongly) called gods.

Whatever the purity of monotheism expressed in these various passages, there is no doubt that the Torah sets forth a radical separation between Yahweh and all else there is. How is this separation to be understood? The chasm that separates Yahweh from all else is predicated upon power or efficacy. Yahweh's fullness of being is based upon the fullness of his creative power, his efficacy. What makes lesser gods lesser is that they are not as powerful as Yahweh.

More power or efficacy equals more being. The creator is always more fully in being than his creation. Whatever efficacy various parts of the creation possess owe to the creator, and are a pale reflection of the creator's own power. Indeed, a truly powerful creator will repeatedly display his efficacy or power. The efficacy of a god who set the world running and then left it to its own devices would be very much in doubt. Is it possible for a people to enter into an intimate relationship with a god who is a "first cause" and who them absents himself from the affairs of the world? Yahweh is certainly no such god. Yahweh is no watchmaker, who sets his creation running according to regular and unchangeable laws. Yahweh is a god who intervenes frequently in the affairs of the world and who offers ongoing and repeated demonstrations of his efficacy.

The first and most fundamental evidence of Yahweh's efficacy is the creation of the world. The formless void, waiting to be acted upon, seems to possess no power or efficacy of its own. It is a blank slate, without any differentiation and thus without any way to be known. If it possesses any degree of being, or efficacy, it is of the most modest sort. The formless void is the recipient, or the medium, of Yahweh's activity. It is passive, lacking the ability to self-actualize or to differentiate itself into meaningful and knowable entities.

In creating the world from the formless void, Yahweh sets apart various beings from one another. He gives these beings form or shape by virtue of their being set apart from one another. This is what it means to create. Nothing in the creation would be what it is if it were not set apart in its being by Yahweh. Creatures derive both their essential beings and also the very possibility of their intelligibility from having been created as they are, and not otherwise, by Yahweh. This may be a matter of fiat, but it is *Yahweh's* fiat and it is to Yahweh that all other beings owe whatever power or efficacy they possess.

Consider Yahweh's first act of world creation, the creation of light. Yahweh separates light from darkness. Both light and darkness derive their meaningfulness from that separation. While Yahweh declares the creation of light to be "good," light does not seem to possess a metaphysical advantage over darkness. Darkness is not, for example, comprehended as the mere absence of light, with light possessing a greater fullness of being. Rather, light and darkness are opposites. It is unclear whether darkness requires a special act of creation to exist, as does light, but darkness and light both derive their intelligibility from their opposition. Light is surely what makes possible the faculty of sight and is thus the pre-condition for human activity in the world. But light is not understood as the medium through which reality becomes as it is. Light possesses no efficacy in and of itself, but is Yahweh's creative backdrop within which lesser parts of creation express their own limited efficacy.

As with light and darkness, so too with every other instance of Yahweh's creation. Yahweh separates dry land and the seas from one another. All of the living creatures of Yahweh's efficacy are created separate from one another. The animals, the creatures of the sea, the trees and the plants – each is created "according to its kind." Lest this point be missed, it is repeated no less than five times in the first chapter of Genesis (at Genesis 1:11, 12, 21, 24 and 25). The kinds of living beings that comprise Yahweh's creation are separate from one another and each recreates itself from its own lineage. Each does so as a pure creation, unmixed with other types, each from its own seed. Each kind owes its unique essence and its intelligibility as a kind to Yahweh.

This point is further reinforced in the second creation account in Genesis. Here it is said that human beings give names to the living creatures of Yahweh's handiwork: "The Lord God... brought each to the human to see what he would call it, and whatever the human called a living creature, that was its name" (Genesis 2:19). This passage makes clear that names are human conventions and that unlike the fanciful suggestion in Plato's *Cratylus*, what humans choose to name things is more or less arbitrary. But while humans name the creatures, it is Yahweh who creates them as they are. The differences among creatures are not merely arbitrary, not merely conventional, and not a humanly constructed morphology.[*] Humans cannot abolish the reality of difference by the words we use to name or to classify. The kinds of creatures which exist are *given* by Yahweh.

Among living creatures the human creature is specially set apart. The human creature is set apart by virtue of being created, in that mysterious phrase, "in the image of" Yahweh. Yahweh gives the human creature "dominion" over all other creatures, which means that Yahweh gives greater power or efficacy to humans than to other living creatures. This dominion appears at first rather benign, until humans rebel and eat from the tree of knowledge. Eating from the tree of knowledge expresses the separateness which the human creature feels – and which then is deepened – from the rest of Yahweh's creation.

For all living creatures, Yahweh sets out a clear and permanent differentiation between males and females. Though in the second creation account woman is created from the body of man, presumably suggesting some underlying commonality between the sexes, a clear and forceful distinction between male and female begins in Genesis and continues throughout the Torah. This disjunction becomes the source of numerous prescriptions, prohibitions, and rituals – each of which is designed to reinforce the distinction itself. The familiar words of the modern marriage ceremony include the injunction that what God joins together, no man should put asunder. The cardinal premise of the Torah might be said thus: what God has put asunder, let no man join together.

---

[*] Samuel Johnson says in the preface to his dictionary, "I am not so lost in lexicography as to forget that words are the daughters of man, and that things are the sons of heaven."

The familial life of the first chapter of Genesis quickly gives way to the organization of humans into peoples or tribes. The universalism of the early chapters of Genesis disappears and becomes an account of the specific lineage, or tribe, of Abraham which becomes Israel.* The people of the world become the peoples of the world, and Israel comes into existence by virtue of Abraham being "set apart" by Yahweh. What is the meaning of this? Why did not Yahweh offer himself as the god of all humans, but choose instead to favor the tribe of Israel? Why has Yahweh chosen Israel and set it apart from other peoples? Is it because of the superior virtue of the people of Israel? Such an argument is never made in the Torah. Indeed, the books of Moses suggest again and again that the people of Israel do not possess an intrinsic virtue, independent of Yahweh, which Yahweh finds attractive. The text refers repeatedly to the tribe of Israel as a proud "stiff-necked" people. They are a people given over to endless temptations. They are a people who, during even the temporary absence of Moses, make all the wrong choices. They are a people tempted again and again by the women, the practices, and the gods of their neighbors.

If not more virtuous, are the people of Israel wiser than other peoples? Stronger than other peoples? More ancient than other peoples? None of these is anywhere offered as a reason why Yahweh has chosen Israel as his own. Indeed, nowhere in the books of Moses is there ever advanced *any* reason why Yahweh has chosen Israel. Perhaps it might be thought impertinent to speculate about Yahweh's motives in choosing Israel. But the books of Moses are replete with statements, inferences, and speculation about Yahweh's motives in other instances. Upon the principal question of why the grace of

* This is why in the Christian view Jesus becomes the second Adam, not the second Abraham.

Yahweh should have fallen upon Israel, we are left to suppose that Yahweh had his own reasons, reasons which he has kept to himself.

Why in turn has Israel chosen to worship Yahweh? Is this simply a response to Yahweh's choice of Israel? In part the choice seems thoroughly pragmatic: when Israel chooses Yahweh, it prospers and its enemies are defeated; when Israel turns away from Yahweh, it suffers. This is a conditional covenant: Yahweh rewards and punishes. For Israel to remain faithful to Yahweh seems to require that Yahweh demonstrate this conditional covenant from time to time. Yahweh must demonstrate his power to the people of Israel. He must reveal his presence in tangible ways throughout the wandering in the wilderness, and he must display his power in defeating the fearsome inhabitants of the promised land. As a practical matter, the people of Israel require occasional demonstrations of Yahweh's power in order to sustain their faithfulness to Yahweh.

But there is a deeper covenant which Yahweh has made with Israel. Like a patient parent, Yahweh is determined to remain with his choice of Israel no matter how faithless are Israel's choices. This choice is made when Yahweh "sets apart" Abraham. Yahweh chooses the blood line of Abraham to favor as his own. As an empirical matter, direct lineage or descent from Abraham is what sets Israel apart from all other nations (Genesis 15:2-4, 21:11-13, 24:7). Lineage establishes the terms for membership in the tribe favored by Yahweh.* It is not as an individual, but as a member of the tribe of Israel – the lineage of Abraham – that one comes under the favor of Yahweh.

---

* To speak to this, Matthew begins his gospel by tracing the lineage of Jesus back to David, and thus all the way back to Abraham – even though this is the lineage of Joseph, who only married the biological mother of Jesus.

This "setting apart" is repeated throughout the books of Moses. Joseph is "set apart" from his brothers and sold into Egyptian captivity – in order eventually to permit the lineage of Abraham to survive as a people. In Exodus, the setting apart is drawn specifically between Israel and Egypt. Indeed, many of the miracles performed in Egypt seem to have as their primary rationale to make clear to both Israelites and Egyptians the power or efficacy of Yahweh. This is the case with the final Passover act, which is done so "that you may know how the Lord sets apart Egypt and Israel" (Exodus 11:7).

By the 33rd chapter of Exodus the distinction between Israel and Egypt is generalized. Henceforth Israel is to be understood as distinct not only from Egypt but from all other peoples. At Leviticus 20:24 Yahweh says "I am the Lord your God who set you apart from the peoples." This is reaffirmed at Deuteronomy 10:15, where Yahweh is said to have chosen the seed of Israel's fathers "from all the peoples." This separation is confirmed from the outside; Balaam says of Israel that it is "a people that dwells apart" (Numbers 23:9).

But lineage is not the entire story. For although it is lineage which sets the tribe of Israel apart in practice, it is the relationship with Yahweh that confers importance or meaning upon being set apart. It is asked at Deuteronomy 4:33 whether any other people has heard a voice like Yahweh's or experienced the deeds he has done. If the people of Israel do not hear the voice of Yahweh, what is the importance of their being set apart? What could be the meaning of lineage for a people who do not witness and are not moved by the power of Yahweh? Moses makes this point forcefully when he asks Yahweh "Will it not be by your going with us, that I and your people may be distinguished from every people that is on the face of the earth?" (Exodus 33:16). If Yahweh is not present, Moses loses his authority. But even more, if Yahweh is not present, Israel loses its distinction as a people. It is the mutual choice of Yahweh and Israel for one another which sets apart the tribe of Israel from all other peoples and which confers meaning and value to the seed of Abraham.

Adam and Eve enjoyed an intimate, personal relationship with Yahweh. Yahweh spoke directly to them and they to him. This kind of relationship continues throughout the books of Moses – not with all humans, but usually with exceptional humans. Noah is one such person, and Abraham is another. The most significant, of course, is Moses who converses frequently with Yahweh. But Yahweh does not speak directly with ordinary humans, whether members of the tribe of Israel or otherwise. Yahweh displays signs of his efficacy that are available for all, but they become rarer and they come in forms that require interpretation. Yahweh's relationship with individuals is over time increasingly mediated by Moses and by the handful of others who experience a direct relationship with Yahweh. What is implied in this is not that a relationship with Yahweh is unimportant – but that a direct, non-mediated relationship is neither possible nor important for all but a handful of leaders of the tribe of Israel. Members of the tribe of Israel find their relationship to Yahweh in a mediated, social setting. It is as members of the tribe, and not as individuals, that they find their meaning and their role. What is said, in short, is that it is the tribe which has a direct relationship with Yahweh, not every individual member of that tribe. And the head of the tribe, Moses the lawgiver – who does speak directly with Yahweh – does so not in order to fulfill his own humanity, but to bring Yahweh's words and commands to the people of Israel.

Herein lie the depth and force of the strict requirements to divide the clean from the unclean, the legal from the illegal, and the holy from the profane. Each such requirement no doubt had its specific origin and rationale, some of which are lost to us and others which we may only partially understand. But as a general matter, in these strictures we are looking at the core of what makes possible the separateness, and therefore the meaningfulness, of the people of Israel. The very meaning of what is holy (*kadosh*) is that which is divided or set apart. To be "holy" *means* to be set apart from what is common or profane. If (as a pantheist might assert) all the world is god, how could any specific act or practice or artifact be holy? If all the world is god, no part possesses any more or less worth than another. As Schopenhauer remarks in "A Few Words on Pantheism," if one begins with the world and then asserts that the world is god, one has added no new understanding about the world. Where nothing is profane, nothing can be holy; the orientation of pantheism makes no discrimination possible.

The practice of setting apart the holy and the profane may, as Alter suggests, reflect a fear of disorder and chaos. But it is more than that. If nothing is holy or set apart, the people of Israel cannot be set apart. The people of Israel maintain the very possibility of their identity in the preservation of the holy. More than psychological reassurance is lost if it is not possible to distinguish the holy from the profane; what is lost is the distinguishing characteristic of the people of Israel.

A tribe living by itself in a remote corner of the world could perhaps attenuate its emphasis on the holy. But a tribe like Israel, which came into continual contact with its neighbors, seemed to require an elaborate and nuanced set of rules by which to set apart the holy from the profane – and thus to set itself apart as well. The very practice of following these rules – as opposed to the intellectual rationale for the rules – makes possible the meaningful continuation of the people of Israel. Yahweh says to Israel "you shall be holy, for I am holy" (Leviticus 11:45). If Yahweh is not holy, that is, set apart,

Israel cannot be holy; and if Israel is not holy, wherein lies the human meaning of Yahweh's holiness? Yahweh's efficacy can have no earthly meaning if no people sets him apart as holy. Thus is set up for Israel "a perpetual statute for your generations, to divide between the holy and the profane, and between the unclean and the clean, and to teach the Israelites all the statutes that the Lord spoke to them by the hand of Moses" (Leviticus 10:9-10). To do less would be to obliterate the very meaning of the tribe of Israel.

Permanence of Kind and the Immortality of the Tribe

The kinds of beings which exist are fixed by Yahweh. This is not to say that Yahweh might not have created other kinds of beings, or that he might not still destroy existing kinds of beings or create new ones altogether. Why should anyone, least of all the people of Israel, question Yahweh's power to do such things? For the people of Israel, Yahweh's intervention was possible at any moment. Indeed, as we have seen, Yahweh's occasional intervention seemed necessary to confirm his continuing power or efficacy. Patterns of growth and decay, of night and day, and the coming of the seasons were regular and discernable; but the world was by no means the world of mechanical laws postulated by a 17th century deist. Yahweh's intervention was possible at any time; victories and defeats were ascribed not to a mechanistic operation of natural forces, but to Yahweh's blessings or curses.

The world is a contingent entity; it is as it is because Yahweh made it so and not otherwise. But it is decidedly not a world of human contingency. Yahweh might intervene in the affairs of the world at any moment – but it is Yahweh, and not human beings, who has this power.* The kinds of beings which

---

* Yahweh pledged to limit his intervention, and thus the contingency of the world, in only one way. He pledged never again to destroy all living

exist are not merely human or conventional realities, but the creations of Yahweh. While humans are the most powerful of all living beings, the stricture on humans is that they must operate within the context of the kinds of beings which are created by Yahweh. Humans are to acknowledge, to accept, and to defend the separateness of the kinds of beings which Yahweh has created. For human beings to confuse, or worse yet try to obliterate, the kinds of beings which exist is tantamount to obliterating the most important distinction of all: it is for humans to try to become like Yahweh. It is the power to create *kinds* of beings which is the core of Yahweh's – or any god's – power.[*]

This point is made repeatedly in the books of Moses, beginning with the fall in Eden. By eating from the tree of knowledge, humans aim to transcend their station and to assume the latitude of Yahweh. When they do, Yahweh punishes them in the most appropriate way: by imposing new limitations on their capabilities. This point is also made in the otherwise inexplicable account of the "sons of god" mating with the "daughters of man" (Genesis 6:1-4). The mating of gods and humans, so common in Greek and other mythologies, breaks down the distinction between gods and humans. Yahweh again reinforces human limitations as a result. It is the

---

creatures as he did with the flood. The world and its seasons will last forever (Genesis 8:21-22 and 9:8-17).

[*] An interesting incident occurs as Moses announces one of the plagues on Egypt. Moses and Aaron use Yahweh's power to turn Aaron's staff into a snake. But the Egyptian priests are able to turn their staffs into snakes as well (Exodus 7:8-13). Where the power to turn one kind of being into another is present, there the gods are present. When the Christian wafer becomes body and the wine blood, this is evidence that a god is present. In later times the "shape shifting" of pagans was firmly read out of the church; if one being can become a different kind of being, divine power is at hand, and shape shifting blurs the hard and fast distinctions between kinds of beings.

proper role of human beings to accept and defend the distinctions which Yahweh has created. It is impure and detestable that what is set apart should comingle, or blend, or cross over the divide between the kinds of beings which Yahweh has created (Deuteronomy 22:5, 9, 10, 11). It is not for humans to try to improve on Yahweh's work by bringing together what Yahweh has set apart; to do so is to seek to become like Yahweh.

In all this, it is not the specific individual or creature which is at stake. It is the preservation of the separateness of kind which is at stake in the books of Moses. The specific creature is of little account so long as the *kind* is maintained. For the people of Israel, it is the tribe of Israel which is primary and through which the relationship with Yahweh is validated or challenged. It is the preservation of the tribe which is at stake. The tribe seeks to preserve itself in its exile in Egypt, through its wandering in the wilderness, and in its later exile in Babylon. It is probable that many members of the tribe of Israel did not go to Egypt or to Babylon, and certain that many new members were born in both places. Individuals may come and go, but the tribe or the people is what is significant.

It has often been remarked that there is no emphasis on proselytizing or conversion to faith in Yahweh, and that historically conversion to Judaism has been quite difficult. There is a strong hint of this at Genesis 34, which recounts the story of Dinah's assault by Schechem. Schechem and his tribe agree to undergo the tribe of Israel's demand to be circumcised in order to keep Dinah, and perhaps even to inter-marry the two tribes to create a union. But accepting this practice of the tribe is clearly insufficient, for Schechem and his tribe are slaughtered to the last man by the sons of Jacob. The offense against the bloodline of Israel clearly trumps the adoption of Israel's rites by outsiders.

From time to time, individuals – and particularly women, such as Ruth – become assimilated to the tribe of Israel, demonstrating that the purity of lineage is not all that is at stake. But as a general proposition, what is at issue is the preservation of the tribe, and so long as that occurs, adding new members to the tribe is somewhat beside the point. Indeed, what value could conversion to the tribe of Israel hold, either for the converted or for the tribe? For the converted, only that they might marry and satisfy a personal, temporal wish. For the tribe, not even that. Where the immortal fate of individuals is at stake, conversion religions make sense and proselytizing becomes an arguable duty. Where this is not so, there is no meaningful rationale for proselytizing.

The coming and going of individuals who are members of the tribe of Israel is of small consequence. There is no personal immortality to be found in the books of Moses. What is – or at least can be – immortal is the tribe, and whatever share of immortality one can attain derives from one's membership in the persisting temporal chain which is the tribe. No "part" of individuals will survive their physical death; indeed, there is no significant sense of discrete "parts" of individual humans, like body and soul, anywhere to be found in the books of Moses.

What "parts" are discussed are the "parts" of the tribe – where individuals are set apart as priests, or warriors, or herders. There is no Platonic reflection of these "parts" of the tribe within individual human beings, as is proposed in the *Republic*. There is no sense of a "priestly part," or a "warrior part," or a "herder part" of individual members of the tribe – these are simply roles performed within the tribe.

Nor is there advanced a clear sense of personal deliberation in the books of Moses. To be sure, there are occasions where one finds something approximating human deliberation. Abram surely hesitated – one supposes he hesitated – before agreeing to sacrifice Isaac. And Moses asks Yahweh why he of all people should be called by Yahweh to lead the people of Israel. But the sense of deliberation is very attenuated; it is nowhere presented as a struggle between human faculties such as reason and passion, heart and head. Individuals are called to act, and to be called is to be under the sway of an outside power greater than oneself, a power which cannot successfully be resisted. No human "faculty" could control such powers; indeed, so little were powerful emotions able to be controlled, they were often ascribed to the gods.

This is not to say that members of the tribe could not, and did not, disregard the commands of Yahweh. After all, the commandments delivered from Sinai speak to individuals of the tribe, and it is the purpose of the teachings given by Moses to conform the practices of members to the rules of the tribe. But one would look in vain to find in the books of Moses a notion of divine justice which operates at the level of individuals. In the later book of Ezekiel, which is perhaps the most "individualistic" book of the Hebrew Bible, it is suggested that Yahweh deals justly with each individual. Without an afterlife, such a suggestion flies in the face of its obvious untruth, at least by any human standard of justice.

The books of Moses root the issue of divine reward and punishment firmly at the level of the tribe. This allows us to understand what strikes many contemporary readers as an unjust and even bizarre characteristic of Yahweh's punishment: the punishment of succeeding generations for the sins of their parents. Exodus 20:5-6 reads: "...I am the Lord your God, a jealous god, reckoning the crime of fathers with sons, with the third generation and with the fourth, for My foes, and doing kindness to the thousandth generation for My friends and for those who keep My commands." This passage is repeated at Numbers 14:18 and again at Deuteronomy 5: 9-10. Indeed, its lesson is already operative in the story of Adam and Eve. For the transgressions of this one couple, Yahweh punishes the human race forever. It is also at work in the story of the flood, where one must suppose there existed such a bright line between the virtues of Noah and the unspecified vices of every other living creature that only Noah, his family, and the creatures he selected for the ark should be spared extermination. It is operative again at Genesis 9, where Ham saw his father in his "nakedness." For this transgression Noah curses not Ham, but Ham's son Canaan. It is operative in the plagues in Egypt, and especially in the slaughter of Egyptian first born males. Here one would have to impute guilt to every single Egyptian family, no matter how low a rank, and then to suppose that justice is served by killing not the parents but their obviously innocent children. And it is operative in granting the land of Canaan to Abraham and his seed. At times the grant of the promised land in perpetuity is laid to the "evils" of its Canaanite inhabitants. At other times, given the manifest iniquities of the tribe of Israel itself, Yahweh grants the promised land to Israel for no very clear reason at all. And in any event, the evils of the Canaanites must be so thorough-going and so widespread as to justify Yahweh's command to the people of Israel to kill every living being in the promised land. Among the various prohibitions found in Deuteronomy 23, Yahweh on occasion reaches well beyond the third and fourth generations: "No misbegotten [of an incestuous union] shall come into the Lord's assembly. Even his tenth generation shall not come into the Lord's assembly" (Deuteronomy 23:3).

What are we to make of this? What are we to make of a god who punishes children to the first, the third and fourth, and the tenth generations for actions that occurred before they were born? Or who punishes whole cities or the entire human species for the actions of some? Exodus 20: 6 says that obedience will be rewarded many times more than disobedience will be punished. Does this make punishment to the third and fourth generations more understandable? And why precisely to the third and fourth generations? Are these passages intended to be literally true, that as an empirical matter Yahweh's punishments will reach precisely so many generations and no further? Contemporary commentators have offered several possible explanations for the punishment of offspring. One is that perhaps a genetic flaw in a perpetrator of evil will also be found in his descendants, at least for a number of generations. Another suggests that children tend to follow in their parents' footsteps and so continue to perpetuate the vices of the parents. Another contends that because the books of Moses offer no personal immortality, one lifetime is insufficient recompense for some acts of evil. Perhaps, too, a transgressor will suffer more deeply if his offspring are punished. Though this may not always be true, it is through one's progeny that one finds such relative immortality as is possible.

Each of these is a valiant effort to make sense of Yahweh's punishments – but from a contemporary individualist notion of justice which misses the fundamental point of the teaching. Each rests on the fundamental contemporary sense that it is inappropriate to punish offspring for the actions of their ancestors. Nowhere is this contemporary sense better expressed than in the American Constitution. Article III, Section 3 reads: "…but no attainder of Treason shall work Corruption of Blood, or forfeiture except during the life of the Person attainted." Punishment – even for treason, which is an attack on the political order itself – shall extend only to the perpetrator and not to his offspring. Why does Yahweh not discriminate at least this finely, that offspring will not be culpable for sins which their ancestors committed?

Moses conducts several interesting conversations with Yahweh about guilt and punishment. In each instance Moses comes across as a man who seeks to tie Yahweh's punishments more closely to the specific individuals who have disobeyed him. Moses negotiates with Yahweh, securing Yahweh's agreement to punish fewer Israelites for the disobedience of some. In Exodus 32, Moses implores Yahweh not to kill all the Israelites because some have disobeyed. He trades on what could only be described as Yahweh's vanity, suggesting that killing every Israelite would serve only to vindicate Egypt. At Numbers 16 and 17, Moses pleads with Yahweh for lenience, and Yahweh agrees to temper his punishment, killing only 250 families, or 14,700 Israelites in all.

In tempering the wrath of Yahweh, Moses comes across as an advocate for mercy for the people of Israel. But for his part, Yahweh makes crystal clear that punishment will *not* be meted out to discrete individuals for their specific offenses. Rewards and punishments are meted out to the tribe, and the consequences that fall upon specific individuals – or their offspring – are of no great account. The fate of particular individuals is not the relevant consideration. Yahweh is the school master who holds the entire class accountable for the actions of each of its members. The force of the book of Moses – spelled out most thoroughly, even laboriously, in Leviticus, Numbers, and Deuteronomy – is that blessings and curses, rewards and punishments, operate at the level of the tribe and can be understood only at the level of the tribe. Deuteronomy is one long paean to the persisting entity which is the tribe. Blessings and curses are meted out to the entire people of Israel (Deuteronomy 28, Leviticus 26) and guilt is fixed at the level of the tribe (Numbers 15:14). Nor does the guilt of the tribe require conscious intent to disobey the commands of Yahweh. Any divergence from the commands of Yahweh is a sin, and ignorance of Yahweh's commands is no justification. The tribe can sin unintentionally (Leviticus 4:5, 4:13, and 10:17) and accordingly deserve Yahweh's punishment.

So long as we aim to force this tribal ethos into the conventions of contemporary individualism, we will make no sense of it. Its teachings will seem incoherent and arbitrary. If, however, we begin with the premise which Yahweh himself repeats again and again – namely, that his justice operates at the level of the tribe – we will achieve a clearer understanding. This understanding may not be congruent with contemporary notions, but Yahweh's plain words need not be tortured beyond all recognition to be comprehended. So long as the tribe persists, the tribe will justify Yahweh's commands and, in a way, even Yahweh's efficacy, that is, the fact that he has chosen to favor Israel. What is lost in this, of course, is the current prejudice to find the origins of modern individualism in the Hebrew Bible. The regime that is presented in the books of Moses is a thoroughgoing theocracy, without the barest hint of limited government or the rights of man. It is a regime dictated by Yahweh and the interpreters of Yahweh's words are the arbiters of the tribe's actions.

In all of this, our contemporary concept of time is collapsed. The persistence of the tribe is the goal, and it is no concern if members of the tribe are punished in greater or smaller numbers, now or in following generations. What happens to the tribe happens to the tribe, and justice is not affected whether the consequences of sin fall now or upon succeeding generations. To make the point as clearly as possible: when the tribe is key, it is no more unjust that the third and fourth generations be punished for an act of the first, than that today's murderer be punished whether he is caught promptly or only after a lengthy delay.

Morality and Justice of the Tribe

If Yahweh's justice operates at the tribal level, how are we to understand what is ethical or moral behavior for members of the tribe? Here again we must set aside contemporary individualistic assumptions. When we think today of "ethics" we think of rules for individuals to follow in making choices about specific decisions or courses of action. These rules are to guide, or at least to clarify, the choices which an individual makes. They are also to be valid universally, that is, the rules will point to the same outcome if one confronts the same choice at another time and place. They are also universally valid in that they will point to the same outcome for different individuals who find themselves in the same situation.

This understanding turns the original meaning of ethics completely on its head. In aiming to abstract, to universalize and at once to apply general rules to discrete choices, ethics is now tortured so far from its original sense as to render it virtually meaningless as an enterprise. This, by the way, is why there are so many quagmires and such little clear guidance to be found in contemporary ethics courses.

To approach the original, tribal understanding of ethics, let us consider the English equivalent of *hivdil*, which is so critical in the books of Moses – the word "kind." When we say that someone is "kind," we mean that he or she is motivated by a favorable sentiment or by good will toward others. We mean that he or she cares about others and displays an interest or sympathy in their well-being. This, however, is a relatively recent usage. The word "kind" derives from the old English "*gecynd*," which in turn derives from the Aryen "*gen*," "*gon*," or "*gin*." This is also the root of "gens" or "genus," which means type. This is the sense of using "genus" as "kind," as in what *kind* of animal is that?

There is a close and understandable relation between these

two uses of the word "kind." The root of "gen" signifies begetting or giving birth. It signifies birth, origin, engendering – from which are derived the words "genes" and "genesis." Genesis is not merely that which is first; it is that which gives birth to what comes later. As Alter says, the primeval Hebrew history is a record of archetypal fathers. One's "kind" are those related by blood, by lineage, by birth. This is the sense of the truncated form of "kind" which survives in a somewhat dated fashion as "kin." One's kin are those with whom one shares a blood relationship.

The implication is clear enough: it is normal, or natural, to have sympathy toward those to whom one is related by blood. The young of an animal were called "kindle," which as a verb means "to give birth to." A now unused word, "kindless," meant to be lacking in natural power or feeling. One is *kind* – in its double sense, this says it all. To whom is kindness shown? The question resolves itself into another: who is one's kind? How far does kindness reach? The original question of ethics is to know who is, and who is not, one's kind.

Now it is obvious that individuals can and do sometimes demonstrate great unkindness toward their own kin. Murder occurs very early in the first chapters of Genesis, and it is the murder of a brother by a brother. Moreover, it is of course possible to show a measure of kindness to those beyond one's kind, and the books of Moses offer several strictures as to how to treat outsiders who live among the tribe of Israel. It is not that the normal cannot be contravened, but rather that what is normal is love of one's own – kind. The punishment for murder of one's own – and particularly of fathers – is, for that reason, very harsh.

Knowing one's own is the origin of ethics. This is expressed in the Greek word "ethos" from which is derived the word "ethics." Ethos does not refer to a specific choice or action of an individual; the ethos of a people is its character which is displayed through time. Ethos is no happenstance possession of an individual, even of a great leader of a people. Ethos is what reflects the prevalent force or attitude or sentiment of a tribe or a people. In a manner of speaking, it is a Weberian "ideal type" of a tribe or a people. Ethos is not a set of rules which transcends the norms of a people; it is the expression of these norms. Though the great leader differs from the ordinary man, he is not a complete outsider. He does not create a newly invented set of norms, but fulfills the norms of the people. He does not create his own fate, but is called to it by a god. He may be plucked from obscurity to play this role – and the more obscure the better — and to undertake a great or unusual action. But this action is displayed and understood as the fulfillment of the ethos of the tribe.*

Related to "ethos" is "ethnos," or nation. The Latin word for nation derives from *"nasci,"* which means to be born. The related words *"gnasci"* and *"gnatus"* are cognates of "genus." A nation or a people is descended from common birth, often understood literally as a common ancestor or father of his people. The long evolution to our current inverted way of thinking can be traced through the Greek word *"ethnikos,"* which meant to be heathen or of a different nation. In later Greek, *"ta ethne"* referred to those who were outside the circle which included gentiles and Israelites. Early English usage followed this closely: "ethnic" referred to those from pagan nations, who were neither Christian nor Jewish. Today we use the word "ethnic" in completely the opposite way. We have abstracted and generalized the term so there is no connotation of

---

* The Jesus presented by Matthew at 5:17 understands himself in this way: "Think not that I have come to abolish the law and the prophets; I have come not to abolish them but to fulfill them."

insider or outsider; everyone has one or another ethnic background.

Who then is one's kind? One might infer from the early chapters of Genesis that all humans are one's kind. Humans, after all, are descended from Adam and Eve (though Cain's wife appears out of nowhere at Genesis 4:7) – and again from Noah and his family after the deluge. If this were so, humans would all be of the same kin.* But primeval human history quickly gives way in the Torah to the story of Abraham and his lineage. The human family has grown so large and so diverse that it cannot be comprehended as a family. This is arguably the only evolutionary development of any consequence in the books of Moses. Humankind is not abolished, but is separated into tribes and peoples, and members of the tribe realize the fullness of what is possible for them as members of their tribe. From a theological perspective, Yahweh commands this for the people of Israel. From a secular perspective, Yahweh's role is to explain and justify the self-understanding of the Israelites that they are set apart from all other peoples.

It is a very significant transition from the species to the tribe, and one for which the ground was not well prepared in the early chapters of Genesis. One is of course tempted to read the transition backward, as it were, and to see Yahweh's blessings upon Abraham as a justification for the reality of the existence of the tribe of Israel. However this may be, the books

---

* Although contemporary evolutionary theory seems to point increasingly to a single human origin, there is no reason why this should have to be so. More or less similar, perhaps random, approximate types of humans might have arisen on earth. Humans could be only more or less the same, and subject to further evolutionary differentiation at that. No doubt the very powerful tools of modern genetics will make a contribution to this debate. Indeed, it is likely that the genetic make-up of beings will become ever more clearly *the* way in which differences and similarities between humans and other beings will be understood. Ironically, modern genetics may also teach how to create new and only more or less human creatures as well.

of Moses make abundantly clear that the people of Israel are to realize their humanity through their membership in the tribe of Israel. Justice is what conduces to the well-being and the preservation of the tribe of Israel, which fulfills the commands of Yahweh. No more is needed. Indeed, no more is possible. A fully just life requires nothing beyond the tribe.

Where then does morality and justice reside within the tribe? Does justice consist of giving equal to equals – and by implication unequal to unequals? But who is equal and how is equality to be measured? "Equal to equals" is a mathematical phrase; in mathematics any quantity or expression which is equal to another can be freely substituted for it. Nothing is gained or lost in such a substitution. But in what way are people exactly "equal" to one another? Some are old, some children; some men, others women; some strong, others infirm; some full of experience and wisdom, others headstrong and rash. The idea that all humans – or all members of the tribe – are somehow "equal" is a supposition nowhere to be found in the books of Moses. That all men are equal is "self-evident" is powerful political rhetoric, but not at all self-evident to the authors of the books of Moses.

To the contrary, in the books of Moses each group among the tribe is to be treated in its own way. Men and women, priests and non-priests, the holy and the profane – each is treated according to rules appropriate to its type. Shall we then say that morality and justice consist in giving each type its "due?" But "due" is a legal/economic formulation, which presupposes an entire legal system for its content. If what is "due" to another seems obvious, it is only so because we are accustomed to the political/legal/economic structure through which what is "due" is commonly defined. One could reason one's way through the Torah forever and never understand why the precise strictures as to how to treat men and women, priests and ordinary tribal members, are established.

Yet the idea of what is "due" does capture something of the original meaning of justice, if only in an abstracted legal way. It is better to say that the core meaning of justice is doing that which is "appropriate" (*to epiballon* for Stoic philosophers) in a broad way, rather than what is "due." Giving that to which others are entitled, or owed, as Socrates pointed out, is only one way in which giving to others may be appropriate – and indeed may be inappropriate. But what is appropriate? In English, what is appropriate is what is fitting or suitable. Grammatically, "appropriate" derives from the Latin "*ad propriem,*" which is roughly "to make one's own." What is appropriate is what is near to one, what is next to one, what is one's own. The basis of moral or just behavior does not emerge from an abstract judgment about equality or inequality, or from a calculation of what is due to others; it emerges as a natural outpouring of care for what is close, of what belongs together, of what is appropriate. For a member of the tribe, moral or just behavior is rooted in understanding oneself as a member of the tribe and in fulfilling the role that is required by the practices and codes of the tribe.

Here we must be clear. One's own is *not* what belongs to one individually, at the expense of others in the tribe. To think this would be to subscribe unwittingly to the notion that tribal demands are based upon the cynical trickery of priests. It is altogether to the contrary: *what is most fully one's own is what is common, what one shares with others.* What is held in common is one's participation in the tribe. To be akin is to dwell with others. Where and with whom one dwells, there is home, there is kin, there are those with whom one shares not only material goods, but the essence of one's very being. One is defined by membership in the tribe of which one is a part, with which one shares one's life, and which in turn defines one's core being.

For this reason, the harshest penalties against malefactors all cut them off from the life of the tribe. Death is obviously one such penalty, and that is clear enough even to modern individualists. But so, too, is exile. For a class of sins which is serious, but less so than those deserving death, the prescribed punishment is exile. If, for example, one eats blood or fat contrary to the command of Yahweh, the punishment is to be "cut off from his people" (Leviticus 7:25-26, 17:13; 20). If one eats leavened bread, contrary to the command of Yahweh, the punishment is to be "cut off" from Israel (Exodus 12:15). Today we might think of exile as a moderately harsh punishment, in as much it forces one to leave behind what is familiar, but which does not confine like prison. But this vastly understates the force of exile to a member of a tribe. Leave aside the almost certain physical harm of being set apart on one's own. For a person whose essence is found in his participation in the tribe which worships Yahweh, exile is a kind of death sentence which obliterates one's essential being.

The principal question of justice for a member of a tribe is thus not how one reasons one's way to rules to follow in order to choose a course of action. It is to understand what is one's kind. If one knows one's kind, one will obtain all the guidance needed about how to live a just life. If one does not, one cannot know justice, even imperfectly. The question of justice resolves itself into a question of metaphysics: of what kind am I? No knowledge of one's kind, no justice.

A member of a tribe who knows that this membership constitutes his kind will know what is just: it is to follow the rules of the tribe. These rules are said by Yahweh (and might even be) what conduces to the preservation and well-being of the tribe. These rules may offer minimal protections for outsiders (based on some shared qualities, such a being a "sojourner"), but by and large they favor the tribe over outsiders. And what do these tribal rules specify? It almost does not matter; right behavior consists in following the rules, just as they are.

Now it might be objected that this standard offers no way to assess whether the rules of the tribe (or the commands of Yahweh) are themselves "just" in some larger sense. Indeed, this is precisely the criticism that philosophers put to the notion of tribal justice. But here we are already beyond tribal life. It is the role of the tribe to provide an answer to the question of what kinds of beings there are, and to root the essence of tribal members in their participation in the tribe. It should perhaps be said again that the teachings of the books of Moses suggest the need to fortify the tribe against extra-tribal and individualistic tendencies. It is not, after all, as if no Hebrew in Moses' time could have wondered whether each and every command, ritual, and punishment that Yahweh set out was necessary and just. But still and all, defense of the tribe is not the only possible answer to these centrifugal tendencies which raised the question of how life is best lived. Nor is the defense of the tribe and of one's own lineage through the generations the only possible way to understand how best to live.

The Task of Obedience

How then are members of the tribe of Israel to live? The answer to this question is easy to state and difficult to practice. The task of the member of the tribe is to obey the commands of Yahweh. The cardinal virtue taught in the books of Moses is obedience. It is through obedience that one displays one's loyalty to and participation in the tribe, and through which justice is expressed. The lesson of obedience is taught without surcease from the beginning of Genesis to the last page of

Deuteronomy. In the beginning chapters of Genesis, Yahweh tells Adam and Eve not to eat from the tree of knowledge, but never says why. Yahweh does not reason with Adam and Eve. He does not explain why they should not eat from the tree of knowledge. He does not offer even the slightest hint why he sets forth this command. He simply does.

The lesson is clear: what is important for humans to know is the command itself and not its rationale. Perhaps one could argue that prior to gaining knowledge of good and evil, Adam and Eve would have had no way to understand Yahweh's rationale. This, after all, is the event whereby Adam and Eve gain such knowledge. But every later story in the Torah – after which humans do possess self-knowledge – offers the same message. At the time of Yahweh's command to Noah to build an ark, there appeared to be no reason to do so other than Yahweh's command. What is Noah's task? It is not to deliberate upon the reasons for Yahweh's command; it is to obey. At stake in Noah's obedience or disobedience is the survival of the human species.

So, too, with the story of Abram and Isaac. It has often struck followers of the books of Moses as strange that Yahweh would command Abram to sacrifice his son. A doctrine of sacrificing one's first born son is certainly not a universalizable code of conduct that could survive among any people. Indeed, because Isaac is Abram's own son, the command runs quite clearly to the in-appropriate. Indeed, that is just the point: the command is a test, pure and simple, and there is no other lesson than that it is right to obey Yahweh. This point is made again, in a most poignant way, in the story of Job.

But how are Yahweh's commands to be recognized? Yahweh's commands at times can seem quite strange. Yahweh seems not to demonstrate even the barest measure of predictability. He appears when he wishes to appear, and when he does not, his "face remains hidden." Yahweh appears in the most unconventional and unexpected ways – in burning bushes, in pillars of fire, in clouds of smoke, as light itself, or by way of "messengers" who speak on his behalf. Yahweh is known when and only when, where and only where, and how and only how he chooses to be known. His reasons to favor the people of Israel, to free Israel from Egyptian bondage, and to grant Israel the promised land all lay hidden in obscurity. So much less clear are his reasons for treating individual members of the tribe one way or another.

Indeed, no matter how many or how clever the attempts, there is simply no path to reason one's way to a knowledge of Yahweh or his motivations. The most one can say is that some of Yahweh's commands appear to be reasonable by human standards and that others do not. We can interpret and re-interpret Yahweh's commands. We can put them into a context which allows us to make sense of them on some occasions. When we succeed, there is harmony between our human understanding and Yahweh's will. But then come the awful times of real and inexplicable suffering, and of apparent deep injustice, and the human mind cannot seem to fathom the world which Yahweh wills to exist.

To judge Yahweh's commands by human standards is to reduce Yahweh to human dimensions. It is to obliterate the distinction between Yahweh and humanity. Human standards are not the standards by which to measure Yahweh; Yahweh's standards are the standards by which humans are to be measured. Thus, it is always wrong for humans to "test" Yahweh, to make their assent to Yahweh conditional upon his actions. That is to invert the natural order of things. It is Yahweh who tests humans; for humans to test Yahweh is to invert the rules of man and Yahweh (Deuteronomy 6:16).

So much less should humans attempt to emulate Yahweh,

for the attempt to emulate Yahweh is the attempt to become god-like. Testing Yahweh reduces him to human proportions; emulating Yahweh aims to elevate humans to Yahweh's status. The emulation of Yahweh is always and invariably punished in the books of Moses. Adam and Eve are punished when they reason to themselves that they could become more god-like if they ate the fruit of the tree of knowledge. Those who aimed to build a tower at Babel to reach up to the heavens are punished. Humans are to remain within their human horizon. We occasionally hear it said today of good people that they are god-like. This is most emphatically not the counsel of the books of Moses. The task is not to *be* like Yahweh, but to *obey* the commands of Yahweh.

That it offends rather than pleases Yahweh for humans to aim to be god-like raises a difficult theological question. Can human beings by their choices cause Yahweh to be "offended" or "angry" or "pleased?" Can humans control Yahweh, at least to this extent? Do humans have such efficacy that, unlike the other animals of creation, they can move Yahweh to anger, jealousy, or vengeance? Later traditions such as Kabbalah suggest this cannot literally be true, for it would detract from the power and majesty of Yahweh if he could be so easily controlled by human beings. Mystic Kabbalists and those inclined to rationalism both incline to a wholly transcendent Yahweh, spoken of only by negatives – such as that Yahweh is not finite, and so forth. Kabbalists argue that references to Yahweh in the books of Moses are but imperfect human attempts to grasp something of Yahweh through his "emanations," not distinct knowledge of Yahweh himself. But this is a later tradition which seeks to reconcile the revelations of Yahweh with universalistic norms – and which carves away the basis for revelation altogether. About this we need comment no further here, other than to say that this more modern rendering takes us further from, not closer to, the books of Moses. There is certainly no intrinsic reason why a being such as the Yahweh described in the books of Moses could not move about the world as he sees fit, and be relatively more or less pleased or angered by it and the human inhabitants he has created.

Human reason is a tool with which we can accomplish many instrumental ends. We can plant and harvest, we can build, we can heal the sick, and we can do much for the improvement of human life. But we cannot reason our way to Yahweh. The commands of Yahweh are neither revealed in nature nor found in human reflection. The commands of Yahweh regarding rules, rituals, dress codes, animal sacrifice, and all the rest could not conceivably be gleaned from looking at the external world, whether as high as the heavens or across the oceans. They could not conceivably be the result of human introspection, no matter how deep or how thoughtful. Indeed, intellection not founded in faith takes one further from, not closer to, Yahweh. It is not wisdom which leads to the fear of Yahweh. It is the other way around, as is said later in the proverbs of Solomon: "the fear of the Lord is the beginning of wisdom." The life of intellectual inquiry is not the way for human beings to perfect themselves or to realize their full humanity. Nor is a life of continual human self-overcoming the path to fulfillment. As Job later teaches, the way of fulfillment – by which a member of the tribe of Israel achieves his fullest human possibilities – is a life of uncomplaining, uncompromising obedience to Yahweh. In such a life one finds the fullness of what is possible, and through which one expresses one's human essence as a member of the tribe which Yahweh favors and which follows his commands.

But if we cannot reason our way to the will of Yahweh, how are we to know his will? How are we to distinguish the genuine commands of Yahweh from the claims of false prophets? Given that blessings or curses will flow from Yahweh, much is at stake (Leviticus 26 and Deuteronomy 28) in getting this right. How can one know the true commands of Yahweh, if not by the light of human reason? This question is raised pointedly, though answered somewhat obliquely, in the books of Moses. The answer provided in the books of Moses is self-fulfilling: the true commands of Yahweh are revealed in *its* teachings. Through his own words Moses reveals the commands of Yahweh. Here, and only here, are to be found the genuine commands of Yahweh in a world which would otherwise appear to be largely random, indecipherable, and meaningless. Here, and only here, are to be found the teachings which make possible the comprehension of the kinds of beings that exist, why each must be respected and perpetuated just as it is, and thus how to achieve the fullness of what is possible for the kind of being that one is. The words of Moses constitute the whole and entire commands of Yahweh to the people of Israel: "You shall not add to the word that I charge you and you shall not subtract from it..." (Deuteronomy 4:2).

Moses asserts the truth of his own claims. But as we have seen, it is a fair question whether the claims of Moses (or anyone else's) can stand entirely on their own. Moses' claims are, at least to some extent, guaranteed by the signs and the actions of Yahweh. Had Yahweh not delivered the people of Israel from Egypt; had Yahweh not provided many signs of his power during the wilderness years; and had Yahweh not brought the people of Israel successfully into the promised land – the truth of Moses' claims would be uncertain, or at least uncertainly known. Moses' words speak for themselves, but they also carry the force of external guarantees which aim to make them plausible. Were it not for the wondrous signs of Yahweh's efficacy, how could one know that Moses himself was not a false prophet? Can a god who offers no sign whatever of his efficacy command the continuing loyalty and obedience of a people?

But the "signs" of Yahweh are themselves capable of many different interpretations. For example, does the survival of Israel in the wilderness constitute a certain proof of the words of Moses? Does the victory over the Canaanite people constitute unambiguous proof that what Moses says is true? Or are not even more extraordinary signs such as pillars of fire and parting waters required? These are questions which human reason might put to measure the words of Moses; as such, they take us outside the Mosaic teachings.

The Mosaic teachings describe a world created by Yahweh which is full of many different kinds of beings. Reverence for Yahweh requires defending the world which Yahweh has created, not improving upon it. It is the task of each being to perpetuate itself as best it can as an instance of its own kind. The kind of being who is a member of the tribe of Israel fulfills his or her being by obeying the commands of Yahweh. In fulfilling this task, reason is of little use. The words of Moses do not require ingenuity to interpret, for they are readily at hand and simple to understand. Moses says (Deuteronomy 30:11-14):

> For this command which I charge you today is not too wondrous for you nor is it distant. It is not in the heavens, to say 'Who will go up for us to the heavens and take it for us and let us hear it that we may do it?' And it is not beyond the sea, to say, 'Who will cross over for us beyond the sea and take it for us and let us hear it, that we may do it?' But the word is very close to you, in your mouth and in your heart, to do it.

One does not find one's humanity as a member of the tribe

of Israel by searching or by reasoning. One finds one's humanity in worshipping Yahweh and obeying his commands. Thus, after the merits of reason have been duly weighed, a later book (Ecclesiastes 12:13) concludes:

> Now all has been heard; here is the conclusion
> of the matter: fear God and keep his command-
> ments, for this is the whole duty of man.

TWO

SOUL:

ON BEING AN ANCIENT GREEK

Psyche is what constitutes the being of beings
which have the character of living.

Martin Heidegger,
Aristotle's Metaphysics

SOUL:

ON BEING AN ANCIENT GREEK

The ancient Greek world experienced a dizzying array of coming and going, of motion and activity. Theirs was a scene of kaleidoscopic activity, of change, and of growth and decay. Each day Greeks, and especially Greeks of the Athenian polis, encountered not only their fellow citizens, but people from distant locales. Each day they encountered living creatures of all descriptions, even in their cities–domestic animals, wild animals, birds, and omnipresent snakes. Outside their cities lay unknown terrors, including outlaws and wild beasts which could descend upon travelers at any moment. Surrounding the land were the seas, lapping the shores with waves. Above, the winds swirled about, moving trees and plants, and often whipping the seas into a frenzy. And enveloping all were the skies, brightly lit with stars in the clarity of the pre-industrial Mediterranean night. Here, too, all was in constant motion, turning and moving across the heavens. Life and movement were all about.

How is it that such life and movement exists? How can the fullness and variety of life be explained? Are there various kinds or types of life, or is all life, by virtue of being alive somehow the same? And for that matter, what does it mean to be alive? For ordinary Greeks, the gods were invoked to explain all this. Like the Hebrews, the Greeks saw their gods as actively engaged in the affairs of the world. These gods made all that occurs to occur, and no more than the Hebrews would they have thought of their gods as setting the world into motion and then disappearing. Like Yahweh, the gods of the Greeks were not only invoked to explain all that existed; they also provided a means to communicate with, and perhaps even to affect, the forces that shaped the world. They offered a medium by which humans could, perhaps only partially and perhaps only occasionally, demonstrate some degree of efficacy with regard to the deepest forces of the universe. Greeks of different stations and of different temperaments surely subscribed more or less to religious rites as simple, time-honored rituals or as matters of personal faith – but the Greek gods remained everywhere present in the events of the world.

Unlike the tribe of Israel, however, the Greeks understood there to be not one, but many, gods. This offered both advantages and disadvantages. There is certainly explanatory economy in monotheism; all that happens to Israel is a result of Yahweh's blessings or Yahweh's curses. On the other hand, there is a degree of specialization in the world of the gods of Greece. This specialization, which is later replicated in the world of Christian patron saints, offers specific gods as causes of specific kinds of events, and to which to appeal for guidance and intervention. This polytheism encouraged a closer familiarity with the gods than the characteristic abyss between god and men in monotheism. Many of the Greek gods appeared more like super-powered humans than authors of the universe, and the mating of gods and men that was read out of the tribe of Israel was an ongoing part of Greek stories about the gods.

The specialization of the gods provoked the questions that led to what the Greeks thought of as science and which we know as natural philosophy or metaphysics. How and why does the wind blow? Because the god of the winds makes it so. Why is some man wildly angry? Because a god or a demon is compelling his violent outbursts. Such explanations lacked the economy, not to say the majesty, of monotheism; naming each of the various forces that moved the world as a god offered a too easy and ultimately unsatisfying explanation. Such explanations begged the question whether these gods were but names for forces which inhered in the beings themselves. And thus was born the quest for immanent causes which is implicit in every form of philosophy, idealism included. Thus was born the human arrogance to look behind the names of the gods, as it were, to seek to understand what exists and how it is possible that it exists.

Some of the explanations which first philosophers offered are bound to strike us today as largely exercises in giving new names to old causes. In a certain way, this could be said of the concept of "soul" itself, which we will consider in some detail. But it would be very wrong to underestimate the radicalism of this development, which raised questions and issues never addressed, for example, in the Mosaic teachings. Early Greek philosophers aimed to penetrate into the (interior) workings of the cosmos as deeply as possible. They fixed themselves on coming and going, on growth and decay, and on change itself, seeking to know these processes for what they truly are. And Plato surpassed them all, suggesting that the ground for all that comes and goes in the cosmos does not itself come and go, but is permanent, unmoved and unchanging. This bold thought, counter-intuitive as it was, has gripped the intellectual imagination of the West ever since.

What Is Soul?

The Greek philosophers' answer to the mystery of life is *psuche*, or soul. Soul is that by virtue of which living beings are alive. To use an older term, soul is the "principle" of life; it is the being of what is alive, the en-livener of life.

How should we understand this? To begin, we should say that soul as the enlivener of being is a description of the function of soul. Enlivening is what soul does. Soul is what allows for an understanding of why, and how, life is possible. Soul offers an explanation for life. But this begs the further question: what does it mean to be alive? If soul en-livens, just what does it do? What is it for which soul is asked to account?

For the Greeks there are typically two aspects, or two qualities, of life for which soul must account. The first and core element of what it means to be alive involves motion. Beings which are alive are in motion, or at least have the potential for motion even if not actually in motion at every given moment. But motion characterizes many, if not all, beings in the world. Are we to say that all bodies that move are en-souled, or alive? For example, a stone may roll down a hillside. Are we to say that stones are alive? Where do we draw a distinction between life and non-life? Do all kinds of motion indicate life, and if not, which types of motion count as life?

Some Greeks came very close to the notion that any body which moves is ensouled and therefore alive. At fragment #7, for example, Hippias says that the philosopher Thales supposed that all moving bodies were ensouled, a report which Aristotle reiterates in *On the Soul*. If iron filings move when they are near a magnet, is there not some quality or power in them which makes them move, which makes movement possible? Why not call this power a kind of soul? In the *Timeaus*, Plato asserts that each star in the skies is assigned a soul. Elsewhere in the *Timeaus* Plato says that the entire cosmos is en-souled and that its soul stretches throughout the cosmos and envelops its body. The cosmos would thus, through its soul, account for its own motion. A somewhat analogous suggestion is made by Philolaus in fragment #21, "On the Soul," where he says that "the soul of the universe is inspired by the breath of nature." And Plotinus later makes a central future of his thought the idea that soul operates at multiple "levels." He argues that human soul is a "part of" the soul of All which, though cut off from the All, can find redemption when it is rejoined to the soul of All and finds its completion there.

It would be fair to say that Greek thinkers did not draw the type of hard-and-fast distinction we tend to draw between what is alive and what is not, seeing instead a spectrum of more and less life throughout the cosmos. Nevertheless, the customary course for a Greek thinker was to seek a distinction between beings which are alive and those which are not, beings which are en-souled and those which are not. A stone is capable of motion, but somehow only if this motion is caused from "outside," that is, if it is thrown, or blown by the wind, or moved by other stones. This kind of motion seems different from another kind of motion that plants or animals display. A plant or an animal can be moved from the outside just as a stone, for instance by being uprooted and tossed aside. But plants and animals seem capable of another kind of motion, a kind of motion intrinsic to them in a way that a stone's motion is not. It is this intrinsic, more "interior" motion with which life is customarily associated. Here we must take care not to read Aristotle's idea of an unmoved mover back into the general Greek idea of soul. As Aristotle himself argues, his predecessors usually identified soul as a being which itself moves, and in so doing causes the body to move. For the Greeks, life of all kinds – including human life – is a response to outside stimuli. These stimuli may consist of the desire for food or drink, or of heat or cold; they may consist of powerful passions that sweep in from the outside; or they may consist of commands from the gods. Hippias, for example, says at fragment #11 (19), "if a god is at work with a divine power, how can the weaker person resist him?" To be alive is certainly *not* equivalent for the Greeks to being self-moved or the master of one's own fate. Life is present where there is a capacity to receive external stimuli not with complete latitude or freedom, but in a somehow "internalized" fashion.

This "internalized" responsiveness leads us to what the Greeks called "*phusis*." To be alive means not only to be able to be moved about by external forces from moment to moment, but to be able to grow and decay, to respond to external stimuli by changing *within* one's own being over time, and to preserve one's being through reproduction. *Phusis*, or nature as it is often translated, is not to be understood as we think of nature today, as a vast system of forces operating according to (mechanical) laws. It is that which grows and evolves within itself all the while it exists in the world. In this way, it would not be wrong to say that *phusis* and soul speak to the same processes. Heracleitus, for example, says that *phusis* is equivalent to soul substance.

Any being which possesses the capacity for "internal" movement is said to be en-souled. Among such beings many degrees of internal responsiveness are possible. Animals are capable of a fuller range of responsiveness to external stimuli than are plants. Humans are capable of the broadest range of responsiveness to external stimuli, that is, they possess the ability for "interior" movement most fully. But this does not mean that being alive is to be "free." It is to be able to respond, according to one's relative fullness of being, to what comes in from the outside. If one is commanded by the gods, as Hippias says, being alive does not mean that humans can choose to ignore such a command; to the contrary, it means that humans are able to respond to it and to act it out. At fragment #18 (6), Gorgias gives an example of what is meant by this. In discussing Helen, Gorgias offers the possibilities that she acted according to fate, that she was seized by force, or that she acted out of persuasion. Nowhere is it implied that Helen chose "freely" her course of action. Different souls signify differing capacities for interior responsiveness in the kinds of beings which they en-soul. But in every case soul is what makes the being of life possible; indeed, it *is* the being of life.

Accounting for movement, and particularly the interior kind of movement that describes life, is the core function of soul. But there is a second aspect of what it means to be alive in addition to movement, and that is to possess sensation, perception, and thought. A living being can receive certain kinds of stimuli from the external world and not move. One might, for example, perceive the color blue or the presence of a flower, and yet not act upon this perception. In such cases, it seems to everyday good sense – and so it seemed to the Greeks – to accord to such a being the quality of life, even though this capability is neither moving about nor growing or decaying. Thus are sensation, perception and thought understood as indicia of life, and beings which display these capacities are displaying the operation of soul.

Indeed, many Greeks understood sensing, perception and thought as analogous to motion, or even as a special type of motion. Physical motion is visible, but sensing, perception and thought are a kind of "invisible motion." Atomist philosophers drew the connection directly: sensation and perception are described as physical motions which are invisible to the naked human eye. Objects are said to give off "effluences" which, although they cannot be seen, reach the eye and make it possible to see those objects. The motion of these effluences is called perceiving; they travel to the eye and fit themselves into "pores." Non-atomist philosophers also likened perception to a kind of receiving from the external world, not of physical effluences but of more or less indeterminate impressions or data. Perhaps it is difficult (or maybe even impossible) to try to describe the operation of human sensation without recourse to analogy with physical movements in space.

Thinking, too, was conceived analogously to motion, though the analogy is less close. Thinking was called, for example, soul "moving about itself" rather than in the visible, physical world of space and time. Whatever this might mean, thinking was regarded as a kind of activity or motion and therefore as a sign of life. As an activity – even though invisible – thinking is therefore evidence of being en-souled.

This, then, is what soul does: it enables movement, as well as the sensation, perception and thinking which characterize life. But we might also ask in the usual Greek fashion: *what* is soul? Is it in any way like body, or is it altogether different? And if it is different, how can it be understood? The traditional Greek view divided the physical world into four constituents of material being: earth, air, water and fire. This is a perfectly reasonable taxonomy, not more or less *prima facie* worthy than others. Whether this scheme produces useful practical consequences is doubtful, and it certainly lacks the depth, the subtlety and the power of the modern table of the elements. But it is a way for ordinary sense to categorize the beings of the physical world. Both pre- and non-philosophical Greeks and some Greek philosophers described soul as a kind of material being, different from tangible physical objects mainly in its "fineness" or its "thinness" or its "ethereal" quality. As such, soul would be understood as one of, or as an admixture of, the elements of earth, air, water or fire. Different philosophers favored different choices. At fragment #2, Anaximenes says "our soul, being air, holds us together." No less a thinker than Heracleitus asserted (at fragments #12, #36) that soul is vaporized water. And Epicharmes says (at fragment #48) that the fire which is soul comes from the sun. By far the most common view – the conventional wisdom, so to speak – was to identify soul with moist, warm air. This identification reflects very accurately the experience of watching a human being or an animal die. As death occurs, the moist warm air of respiration ceases and the warmth of the body slips away until the body reaches the temperature of, and becomes one with, its surroundings. Yet another description of soul emerged from the experience of bloody, violent death where soul poured out of a dying body. But the customary understanding associated soul, or at least described its what-ness, in terms of moist, warm air. All of these and other understandings of soul are conveniently recounted by Aristotle in *On the Soul*, where he concludes that only the element of earth was without an advocate for the what-ness of soul.

Plato takes a different course: he de-physicalizes soul. In the *Phaedo*, Plato has Socrates advance the notion that soul is not to be thought of in any way as physical or tangible, but rather as a "harmony." This view, which was originally associated with Pythagoras and his followers, argues that harmony is in no way tangible or material, but is a mathematical ratio, which is to say, an idea. Lest too much be concluded from this argument, Plato has Socrates argue elsewhere in the *Phaedo* that soul is not a harmony at all. Whatever one makes of Plato's actual view here, a variant of the idea of soul as harmony was later argued straightforwardly by a number of Hellenistic philosophers who spoke of soul as a "tension" of *pneuma* or spirit. This tension, they argued, differs from being to being: in stones it is called *hexis*; in plants, *phusis*; in animals, *psuche*; and in humans, *nous*.

The idea of soul as the enlivener or mover of body raised a number of difficult subsidiary issues. If soul moves body, does it do so by moving itself? Plato raises this idea in the *Phaedrus*, where Socrates argues that while soul is not "generated," it is self-moved. And of course Aristotle advances the view that while soul does indeed move body, it does not itself move; it is an unmoved mover. For Aristotle, this view answers the question of the origin of motion. If soul itself is in motion, it imparts movement to body analogously to how we conceive any other entity imparting movement to another. Soul's motion moves body, though in the manner of growth and decay, sensation, perception and thinking rather than through external force. But what has this explanation really achieved? From where, in turn, does soul receive *its* impetus, its motion? There is a regress here which, to say the least, is not altogether helpful as an explanatory tool.

This problem of regression is solved if one locates the source of soul's motion within itself. But this in turn raises another difficult set of questions. All movement of physical bodies in the tangible world seems to be the result, either directly or indirectly, of forces outside themselves. Soul alone is accorded a power to move itself. But where does this extraordinary, unique power come from? And how does this unique power translate its activity into the movement of bodies? We are surely in difficult territory here. And in a way, this entire concept seems to take us away from, and not closer to, what we conventionally understand as human. For if soul is what enlivens human beings to be just the way they are, soul is rightly understood as the essence of being human. But ironically, this unmoved mover does not itself seem very human, but rather abstract and impenetrable. The essence of being human seems not to be very human at all. Empedocles had already noted this, when he asserted flatly that human soul is not human at all. The animating power of soul seems to be a power which transcends humanity altogether. Soul, which makes the human being possible, may be thought of at one and the same time as the essence of human being and also as very inhuman altogether.

The Parts of Human Soul

To address this ironic quality of soul, we have to clarify soul's relation to body. But this presupposes a fuller understanding of how soul itself exists. After all, even leaving aside the motion of plants and animals, human soul seems to express itself in many ways. Human beings display manifestly different actions and ways of life. Are each of these caused by different types or kinds of soul – in which case humans might be characterized by multiple souls? Or does a simple and undifferentiated human soul make possible the full variety of ways in which human life is expressed? In that case, one cause would seem to lead to many different outcomes, a matter which would require further explanation. Or is human soul somehow differentiated into separate "parts" or aspects, each of which is responsible for its specific type of human activity?

One can find many instances in Greek literature in which authors suggest that humans are moved about by differing aspects of soul. Souls are employed as *thumos* to explain courage; as *menos* to explain desire; and as *nous* to explain thinking. All might co-exist within the same human being, now one coming to the fore and now another. This is certainly a perfectly reasonable, if not altogether helpful way of understanding the springs of human action. It more or less mirrors the employment of the gods as explanatory powers. Each kind of human action, be it growth, or courage, or thinking – is accounted for by its own soul power. This is a form of explanation in which the transcendent powers of the gods are replaced by the immanent powers of soul, but remain no further developed.

It was the consensus view of Greek thought that each human being is ensouled by one and only one soul. This avoids the problem of explaining how multiple souls might co-exist within each human being. It makes possible an easier answer to the question of what it is by virtue of which each soul is soul. But it begs the question of how a solitary soul can cause differing kinds of human expression and action – and points almost inevitably to the idea that there are differing "parts" or aspects of soul. Epicureans, for example, advance the idea of a quadripartite soul composed of air, fire, pneuma and a nameless point. Lucretius later speaks of a two-part soul which has rational and irrational components, which he calls respectively *animus* and *anima*. In the *Republic* (and also the *Phaedrus* and the *Timeaus*) Plato seems to favorably advance a tripartite soul consisting of appetitive, spirited and rational components. Elsewhere in the *Timeaus* he refers to the parts of soul as passion, sensation and reason. And still elsewhere in the *Timeaus* he says that soul is composed of mortal and immortal parts. And in his exhaustive account of human soul, Aristotle suggests among other things that nutritive, sensing, perceiving and thinking are the principal aspects of human soul, each aspect responsible for its specific kind of effect in human action and thought.

What are we to make of this? For those who held that soul was material or corporeal (though of a special kind), perhaps it would not be strange to think that soul could have "parts." For having "parts" or "components" suggests that soul has a physical quality of extension such that it can be divided. Some thinkers come quite close indeed to this notion. Some suggest (an idea later taken over by Augustine) that "parts" of soul are correlated with and even co-located with parts of the human body. The "lower" the part of soul, the lower in the body it expresses itself. The most base part of soul expresses itself through the desire of the sexual organs; next is that of appetite, which expresses itself through the organs of digestion; next is that of courage or spiritedness, which expresses itself through the heart (we retain this way of speaking to this day); and finally there is found the highest part of soul, which expresses itself through thinking.

But for those who thought soul to be incorporeal, how can soul have "parts?" After all, incorporeal soul cannot be divided like the "parts" of a horse, or a building, or any other corporeal being. The more thoughtful way to speak then, was not to speak of "parts" of soul, which implied extension in space; it was to speak of a unified soul which has differing capabilities or powers. Human soul might exercise its manifold capabilities now in one way and now in another, but all the while it will be unitary soul. Perhaps no one better summarizes this than Plotinus. In a formulation that will sound thoroughly familiar to trinitarian Christians, he says in *Ennead* (II) "soul is one nature in many powers ..."

How then do the aspects of soul, be they called "powers" or parts," work with regard to one another? Do they work harmoniously or are they at war with one another? Do they compete for predominance with one another? If appetite or sexual desire predominates at one moment, surely thinking does not; and vice versa. Plato offers a metaphor by which to explore this. He says that different parts of soul pull a human being in different directions, just as two horses might contend to pull a chariot one way or another. He then suggests that a charioteer is needed to guide the horses and the chariot, and identifies the charioteer with thinking or reason. We shall say more of this in a moment. But here we might note that no matter which part of soul is predominant – be it appetite or spirit or reason – the chariot is always moving in only one or another direction. The whole of the chariot/ driver, that is, the whole of the human being, is at any moment moving in one direction and not several directions at a time. This model is not offered, in short, to explain human "deliberation," going back and forth, or what we might call at times indecision, when all parts of soul are balanced off against one another. It is a model designed to explain human motion and action; it is a model of command. Some part of soul or another is always predominant at any given moment, and this part moves the human being in a definitive way.

This is altogether consistent with the ancient Greek understanding of emotions. As we have said, humans can be moved from the "outside," as it were, by being blown by the wind or pushed by other humans. In these movements one might say that human soul is not involved, or at least is involved only in the way in which any being that is moved is accorded soul. For the Greeks, another impulse to movement comes from emotions. E-motions are powerful forces that come from outside a human being, though they express themselves in human action through soul. They do not come from "within" a person. They are powerful external forces over which humans have at best very limited control. They can be so strong that they "overpower" human beings. They are often pictured as demonic in nature, or sent to humans by demons in the shapes of animals. In these cases soul is what makes it possible for these e-motions to express themselves through human (or even animal) beings. But there is always a sense of just that, namely, it is the emotions which are expressing *themselves* and not the human being through which they are being manifest. Upon this understanding, soul is the medium for the expression of emotions, rather than the source of emotions itself.

But what of the expression of soul which is called thinking? Thinking seems to be a more "interior," more human activity than the expression of emotions which wash through from the outside. Indeed, virtually every Greek thinker understood thinking as the most fully or essentially human expression of soul. Democritus (at fragment #146) says that reason lies within the heart of the soul. Gorgias says that the glory of human soul is …wisdom (fragment #11). Plato says "the one and only existing thing which has the property of acquiring thought is soul" (*Timeaus*). And in his hierarchy of soul Aristotle lists at the top "that part of the soul…which we call mind" (*On The Soul*). Moreover for the Greeks, and for Plato especially, there is a hierarchy based upon the increasing "interiority" of the mental-related capabilities of sensation, perception and thinking. Sensation is direct and never errs; one senses what one senses. Sensation is somewhat like emotion in this way, as it comes from the outside and expresses itself more or less directly through the medium of human soul. At the next level is perception, which is also a more or less direct coming to awareness of what comes in from the outside. At the highest – that is, the most interior level – lies thinking, which makes judgments that go beyond the sensations and perceptions which come into the mind from the outside. Making judgments based on external stimuli constitutes the first activity of thinking. There is enough "interiority" in this capacity to make possible errors and mistakes. One senses what one senses; one even perceives what one perceives; but one can judge in error about what it is that one senses or perceives. One can reason wrongly about the external world. For Plato the highest or most interior level of all is the capacity to think about judgments or ideas themselves, about their being and their relationship with one another. This activity is, in a manner of speaking, the most invisible and least active human capability. It is the human activity least connected with the tangible things and physical motions of the external world. It is an activity – it is the activity – which unlike sensing or perceiving, occupies itself wholly with what is intangible, invisible, and interior – or as we usually say, idea-l.

Yet for all of that, human thinking is not to be understood

as idle speculation unconnected to the external world. Thinking is a directive and determinative human activity; when one is thinking, one is directed in a certain way, and not under the sway of the other "parts" of soul which express desire or spirit, for example. This is an altogether different understanding than the modern view, which is perfectly captured in the notion that reason is and ought always to be, the slave of the passions. For moderns, thinking or reason simply carries out the desires of the passions, with more or less efficiency. Reason itself directs nothing. For the ancient Greeks, however, thinking is a directive, orienting activity; thinking need not toil away to achieve ends which are given to it, but is itself a directive power through which one part of human soul manifests human capacity. Though thinking is not always and at all times directive (to put it mildly), it can be, and as such it displays most fully the capacity of soul unique to human beings and through which human beings exercise and display their most essentially human way of being.

None of this is to suggest that human "freedom" is to be found in thinking, in the sense that moderns understand a concept like "freedom of the will." Thinking is the most interior human activity, the one most detached from the immediacy of the tangible world, but not for all of that necessarily a free activity. Thinking is the most uniquely and distinctly human capacity, but not an activity through which the whole human being is somehow or in some way at liberty to shape his will. Whether we are moved by a more external force such as emotion, which expresses itself through one capacity of soul, or whether we are moved or directed by a more interior capacity of soul such as thinking, we are in every case moved about through one or another capacity of soul. Human soul offers a far wider capacity to act than does any other kind of soul – but it is through soul that these capacities are exercised, and it is unclear where any "freedom" in the modern sense might be located in the medium which is human soul. As Plotinus says, though soul has many powers, it is still of one "nature," and no portion or power of that nature is totally unlike the rest.

In concluding, we might note that much of the Greek discussion of the parts or aspects or powers of soul is thoroughly anthropomorphic. The descriptions of the gods who cause the winds, thunder, and waves, are often drawn with human qualities. But so, too, are the parts of human soul. Parts of soul are said to "work harmoniously" with one another, to "compete" with one another and to "war" with one another. Parts of soul are said to express desire or spirit. All of these, of course, are the everyday words we use to describe human action at the level of the whole human being. They are transferred more or less directly to the "parts" of soul in an effort to describe in some intelligible way the otherwise obscure powers of soul. We might ask whether these anthropomorphisms are helpful explanatory tools, or whether they simply recreate the explanation of human action in a different, more interior locale. Lest we moderns dismiss such explanations too quickly, however, we might observe that most modern explanations of human activity employ a very similar approach. In remarking on Freud's "parts" of the human psyche, for example – the desiring part, or id, the calculating part, or ego, and the censorious part, or superego –Wittgenstein wryly remarks that these creations are given qualities and powers that look suspiciously like those by which we refer to entire human beings and actions. And more recently, of course, we have the amusing account of human behavior motivated by "selfish genes," simply transposing a human quality to a "part" or component of the human being. Though modern science, and modern genetics in particular, may vastly advance our ability to manipulate ourselves and our world, it is doubtful that contemporary anthropomorphism takes our understanding of the what-ness of ourselves any further than did its predecessors.

The Relation of Soul and Body

Human soul is thus an enlivening capacity which in its nature is bound to remain quite obscure. Soul is what makes humans to be human, but this essential quality of being human is not the same as human being. Soul is what makes humans to be human, but is itself an entity which seems quite non-human in its abstracted nature. The reason for this is that the description of human soul is not the full description of human being. For if it is true that human soul can express its powers in many ways, these ways all have one thing in common, namely, they are all expressed through the human body. We may suppose or theorize that some expression of soul is possible unconnected to body – and we will discuss this soon – but all direct evidence we possess suggests that the enlivening power of soul needs some being to enliven, without which it would be even more opaque, expressionless and obscure, if not altogether non-existent.

In the usual accounts, the appetitive power of soul expresses itself through desire of the body, its sexual organs, digestive organs, and so forth. The spirited or courageous power of soul expresses itself through the heart. And the thinking power of soul expresses itself through the mind which, though obviously somehow connected to the head or brain, was rarely given so specific a location by Greek thinkers. How exactly does the en-livening, empowering force of soul work through and express itself through the body? How does soul relate to what seems to be the vehicle of its expression?

It is not unusual for people to speak inexactly and to say

that body and soul are two (or the two) "parts" or "constituents" or "components" of human being, again implying some manner of divisibility of a physical or spatial character. Speaking very loosely – and very misleadingly – it is commonly said that human beings "have" a soul. But who or what is the being that "has" a soul? Who or what is the being who is the happy possessor or owner of soul? This manner of speaking is invariably misleading, as it raises the question of where the soul is to be found, or located, in the being who "has" a soul. If one dissects a human body, one finds a heart, lungs, kidneys, and so forth – but no soul. Despite the hasty modern conclusion that this absence disproves the existence of soul, Greek thinkers were well aware that soul could not be found within the body like organs or bones or flesh. To the contrary, they supposed – even in cases where soul was conceived to be somewhat material in its reality – that soul was "intermixed" with body in a far different manner than are organic body parts. Even "intermixture" suggests some degree of soul-physicality, but the intermixture models are different than the commonsense component model. One variant of the intermixture model of body and soul was that of total fusion, such as occurs when an egg is heated. As an egg is heated, the heat and the egg mix together and the egg is entirely changed. The egg is changed throughout, and it is not possible to "find" the heat in the cooked egg, even though its effect is apparent. A different version of the intermixture model is that of total blending. Here soul is understood analogously to the color purple in wine or the scent in perfume. The color or scent cannot be "found" in any part of the wine or perfume, but suffuses the whole. Now the utility of these and other models often depended on what their authors were trying to demonstrate about soul. For example, there seems to be no way to get the heat "back out" of an egg and to restore the egg to its original condition. This would be a dubious analogy for a thinker trying to show that at death soul separates from body and that either soul or body, or both, are able to return to their original conditions. Perhaps through some chemical process color or scent could be extracted from its medium, offering a better basis on which one might argue for an immortal soul unconnected to body.

At all events, it does no justice to the concept of soul to say that humans *have* a soul. We do not have a soul in the way we have a heart or lungs or kidney. It reflects more accurately the Greek idea of soul to say that humans *are* both body and soul, or that we are en-souled. Such a view is far closer to how we ordinarily refer to emotions today. We typically do not say in English that "we have anger," and then go about looking for where within us we are to find anger's physical location. Rather, we say that "we are angry," suggesting that anger has somehow suffused us and permeates or orients our actions. The modern understanding of how to describe emotions takes us closer to the Greek idea of soul as a suffusing, enlivening power of being human. And in turn the modern understanding of emotions should not then be equated with the Greek understanding of emotions. The phrase "we are angry" does not convey the proper ancient Greek sense of emotion. It would be more accurate to say of the Greek view that "anger has us" rather than that "we are angry." Emotions come in through the outside and overpower humans. They flow into humans with a force that often cannot be resisted. They in-fluence us and we ex-press them. As to soul, if there is any "having" or possession involved, it is that soul has body, not vice versa. Plotinus aims to stress this point when he says, perhaps equally misleadingly, that soul is not "in" body, but body is "in" soul.

Having said that soul has no physical location within body, it is nevertheless the case that there is another sense in which soul does have physical location. After all, soul seems to be co-located *with* body. That is to say, the power which en-souls or moves my body seems to be with, in, or near my body and not someone else's body. So long as a body is alive, soul seems to be present with and through that body. At death, soul is no longer present with body; but in life soul seems inescapably co-located with a discrete physical body that has a place in space and time. And this of course seems to root soul in, or at least near, that body's location in space and time. Soul is thus connected with physical body, but the manner of that connection or relationship is very difficult to describe. The Greeks produced lengthy and often bizarre accounts of the way in which soul and body relate to one another, and the ways in which they respectively affect one another. These included trapped vapors, blinded desires, chaotic motions, intense revolutions, and mismatches in size and strength of souls and bodies. What one should make of these fanciful analogies is a bit hard to say. But one point remains clear: the general rule is that soul is known through its effects, which are expressed by the body.

Soul enlivens body. But the relationship between soul and body is not a one-way relationship, for body affects soul as well. Soul enlivens body and in so doing gains a certain ability to express itself through the body. Philolaus (#22) says that soul "loves" body, because without body soul can make no use of the senses. But more often Greek thinkers suggest that soul pays the greater price in the soul-body relationship. Soul enlivens body, but only at the expense of losing an alleged independence as well as its "own" ends. Democritus (#72), for example, says that the violent desires that are able to be expressed only through body can "blind" the soul. Plato asserts in the *Timeaus* that "so often as soul is bound within a mortal body it becomes at the first irrational." And Plotinus says that when a soul "fastens itself" to a body it loses sight of its "own" aims and partakes of those of the body.

What "ends" could souls have when not joined to bodies? The usual view – given its most complete and thorough, if varied, formulation by Plato – suggests that the most interior of all activities are the soul's true ends. This of course is what is called thinking, the contemplation of the relation of ideas to one another. This is the activity least affected by change-ableness, by coming and going, and by the generation and decay of bodies. Plato says in *Phaedo* that thinking is soul's "own" activity, least mediated by the world of changing bodies in time and space.

However difficult it may be to offer a persuasive account of the exact relationship between soul and body, the main point is clear: in every case human beings are to be understood as both soul and body. Plato says in *Timeaus* that a human being is a living creature which is a compound of soul and body. We humans are both finite and also partake of something which points us beyond this finitude. We are rooted in our bodies and in our times and places, but we are aware of what reaches far beyond our bodies and our times and places. What makes us human is the unique way in which we are ensouled. But our essence as soul is not the totality of human being, even though it points us somewhere beyond our humanity. In *Ennead* (II), Plotinus speaks plainly and forcefully to this when he says "For every man is double, one of him is the sort of compound being and one of him is himself." In so speaking, Plotinus aptly suggests what is true in general of the Greek concept of soul. Soul is the essential quality of the human being. If human beings are more fully to realize their essential character, they will be oriented in such a way that soul can express itself least constrained by the medium of body through which it works. This is all perhaps surprising. For soul is invoked to explain human life, but soul is not equal to human life. The en-livener which is soul seems somehow to have a being in and of itself and this being best expresses itself when connected to, but somehow least connected with body. To express the essence of soul is to express the essence of human being, but not to express the fullness of human being. Acting in accord with their essence takes human beings, then, somewhat beyond their humanity.

Where Do Souls Come From and Where Do They Go?

If soul enjoys a greater or lesser degree of existence and purpose independent of body, in what way can soul exist without body? We might begin by noting that for the Greeks being alive or in motion required an explanation or an account in a way in which being dead or at rest did not. Why should a body at rest require no explanation for what it "does" (that is, rests) while a body in motion does? Life for the Greeks begs an account of itself which non-life does not. It is logically possible to conceive a lifeless body as a body plus a "quieting force" or agent, called by some name or another. In such a case, rest would be a special case of movement, a special case which required a cause or an enabler. Lest this seem far-fetched (and it is surely the ordinary starting point to begin where the Greeks did), it is part and parcel of modern physics to treat neither motion nor rest as a special case, but each as requiring explanation. For the Greeks, however, the explanation of life as motion (and its cousins sensation, perception, and thinking) was the starting point. Soul is the being of beings which are alive.

If soul is that which enlivens beings, where does soul "come from?" How does soul come to be joined to or admixed with bodies? Does soul pre-exist its connection to a body, or does it come into existence the moment it is joined to a body? For

Greek thinkers, where soul comes from is not an idle or useless speculation. In the Christian view which later dominates Western thought, considerably more importance is attached to the question of where souls "go" at death than where they "come from" at conception. This is perhaps natural in light of Christian teachings about salvation and damnation. For Greek thinkers, however, the matter was altogether different. Humans are always and invariably moved about by what comes into them from the outside. Perhaps this movement is caused by an exterior force or perhaps it is mediated by soul. But it is a critical consideration as to what are the external forces shaping a living being, and especially a human being. As the being with the most fulsome ability to respond to what comes in from the outside, great care needs to be taken to shape those forces and influences as much as possible. If external forces are all pressing in one direction, this is the direction which will move a human being. When in the *Republic* Plato outlines, somewhat fancifully to be sure, a political order to shape the external forces which will mold young people, this is not an unusual or unexpected project. To the contrary, for the Greeks the environment is crucial in shaping human beings. Great care must be taken in arranging positive and constructive influences, especially for young people. While we moderns often bemoan the coarseness of our culture and its influence on young people, there always remains implicit in our understanding an ability to surmount one's surroundings by acts of free choice – which tempers to a degree the concern which we might otherwise feel about such influences. For the Greeks, however, the forces and influences that come into human beings and express themselves through soul are of fundamental importance. That said, it would be surprising if were a matter of indifference as to the soul's origin. The Greeks cared as fully about the origin of soul as about soul's fate at death.

   The customary accounts of the origin of souls are given in story form. They are highly imaginative, rely largely on physical analogies, and generally offer – to put it kindly – few if any logical reasons to prefer one to another. The account of Orpheus (#11), for example, suggests that soul surrounds the entire world. It is borne by the winds and it (or a portion of it) enters into discrete bodies when creatures inhale. Though it is not said from where comes this power to inhale – which might itself be thought of as soul – all creatures are using a portion of the energy of the whole in their respiration while they are alive. When respiration ceases for any creature, humans and animals alike, soul is exhaled back into the whole. Empedocles, on the other hand, says that soul falls from above and passes through "all manner of mortal forms." This suggests degrees of "weightiness" by which soul becomes associated with specific bodies.

   These and other such accounts of how soul joins body are found throughout Greek literature. Several are related metaphorically by Plato, each serving some larger Platonic purpose in the dialogue in which it is found. In *Phaedrus* Plato says that before becoming joined to human body, soul "beheld the realities." Elsewhere he plainly imputes "intelligence before birth" to soul. And yet elsewhere he says that prior to joining human body, soul has "glimpsed the *Eidos*," the unchanging reality of full being. In *Meno* Plato has Socrates account for the pre-existence of a knowing soul as a functional or logical necessity – in order to explain the possibility of human knowledge – rather than as a story.

   Each of these Platonic accounts of course describes soul in very human terms, much like a person possessing the faculty of sight, for example. Souls "behold," they "glimpse," and they "know." But if Plato relates these stories about pre-existent soul freely, he also suggests that what is not itself body can have no location in time and space and thus all accounts of "where" soul is before human birth are to be understood allegorically. A true account of soul cannot be (fully) given by pictures or images drawn from the physical world. But it turns out that very little can be said about pre-existent soul if it is *not* "likened" to just these pictures and images. The gist of the Platonic accounts of the pre-existence of soul are consistent with the general Greek view, namely, that an abstracted, intelligible, pure power loses a degree of these qualities when it becomes "bound" to body. What once floated freely becomes bound to what is more narrow, to the specificity of time and place, and to the inevitably discrete character of desire.

The departure of soul from body at death is no easier to describe in a persuasive way. How does soul depart from body? When it departs, does it continue to exist? And if so, where does it "go?" In the stories of Greek authors, soul usually departs the body at death either through the mouth or through a wound. For those who portrayed soul as the moist, warm air of respiration it was understandable that soul would depart the body through exhalation. When one ceases to breathe, the power of soul ceases to mix with body, and body becomes one with its surroundings. For those who portrayed soul as more liquid, often associated with warm blood, soul oozed out of the body in a wound at death. Often, the process by which soul leaves body could take some time rather than occur instantaneously. While Epicurus and his followers asserted that soul dissolves at death, others argued that soul dissolves more slowly. Just as bodies retain their appearance for a time after death, and then dissolve slowly into their elements, so too with the dissolution of soul. In many Greek stories, soul is found frequently to linger around the dead body for a period and only then to depart for good.

If soul "departs" the body and if it retains its existence, at least for a time, where does it go? Greek stories are replete with a special abode for souls after death, a place called Hades. Here souls seem to continue to live in human shapes, though in paler versions which are called shades or shadows. They move about as human shapes, but without the visceral qualities of living humans. They move about as if in a dream or as if they are sleep walking, but lacking most kinds of human sensation. While this way of being never seems very pleasant, neither does anything that looks like physical punishment seem to occur in this abode; genuine physical suffering seems to require fully embodied soul. The principal sense faculty in Greek accounts of the afterlife is that of sight, the least corporeal of the senses. Heracleitus (#63, #98), for example, describes souls in Hades as "watchful" (though in fairness he also attributes to these souls the sense of smell). Philolaus (#22) refers to life after death as incorporeal existence, marked by the shapes of humans without their solidity. In the main, the life of souls in the afterworld is a life that *looks* like human life, but is devoid of great pain or joy, of desire or aversion, of emotions and laughter, and of all the qualities we associate with the human body.

It is standard fare in these accounts that souls in the after-world are able to be "recognized" or identified as their former human selves. Plotinus carefully summarizes the customary Greek view that souls in the afterworld recognize one another. And most curiously, Pythagoras is said to have thought that he recognized the soul of a dog he encountered as the very same soul of a former friend who had died. It is hard to know how such a soul could be "recognized" in a dog, as it surely could not be through the sense of sight. Such a view presses Greek thought in the direction of the Eastern view of soul as pure life force or as contentless monad. After all, if soul can inhabit human or animal bodies (or even plants) wherein lies its uniqueness as a free-standing entity? But even in this story, where "one soul fits all," Pythagoras is able somehow to recognize his particular friend. There remains some residue of uniqueness which is recognizable or identifiable in the soul.

Plato offers sufficiently numerous accounts of soul after death to lead one to suspect that each should be understood as pointing to some lesson he aims to teach in its specific dialogue, rather than as a literal rendering of the afterlife of soul. He says in the *Phaedo,* for example, that at death soul goes "into another place" and elsewhere in that dialogue that "our souls will exist somewhere in another world." He further says that after death soul takes with it "its education and nurture." To add to the complexity of the picture, Plato argues elsewhere in the *Phaedo* that soul becomes too intermixed with body during life to be able to depart entirely from the physical world. He describes a process where soul tries to "escape" the physical world, but is "dragged back" into it. After all this, Plato suggests in the *Phaedo* that none of these accounts should be taken literally.

While the popular Greek view represented souls as "going" to another world, and while this view had its philosophical adherents, other philosophers argued that soul does not persist beyond the death of the body. Plato himself proposes a version of this view in the *Phaedo* where he discusses the soul as a "harmony." When the body's vitality ends at death, harmony ends too. This suggests that soul requires body to exist every bit as much as body requires soul to live. Aristotle advances this view most fully and most thoughtfully. For Aristotle, there is no place for soul after death. Aristotle says that soul is the "actuality of a body potentially possessing life," and as such soul requires body as much as body requires soul. While soul is not body, soul cannot exist without body. The dissolution of soul and body is the dissolution of both soul and body, which require one another for their being. This is one reason that later Christian thinkers found favor with Aristotle, who seemed to offer a way of thinking which was at least consistent with the importance of physical resurrection. Aristotle's fully immanent account of soul asks how potentiality becomes actuality. Why do bodies that have the potential to live actually become alive? Why does potentiality turn into actuality? By what power or grace can this occur? All that seems able to be said is that soul is the actuality of a potentially living being.

We might ask what we are to conclude about all these comings and goings of soul before birth and after death. In the main, the Greek view suggests that while humans are to be thought of as both body and soul, and that body and soul differ from one another, each is able to and does affect the other during life. This mutual enlivening by soul and narrowing by body describes the human being. To the extent that human beings are rooted in time and space, and to the extent that soul must express its enlivening powers through the organs of the human body, to that same extent will soul orient itself to the discrete, the particular, the present, and the here and now. To the extent that these limitations are able to be cast off by death – or even to some degree in life, in thinking – to that same extent will soul be able to express itself more abstractly and more generally. But then soul seems to lose its individuality; a soul which does nothing but contemplate ideas would seem to be very much the same as any other soul which contemplates ideas. In life, there is little danger that soul will be able to free itself from body and lose its individuality. Even in death, for most Greeks some degree of individuality is preserved in the shadows of the afterlife. Some aspect of the finitude, the imperfection, and the limitation which characterizes the human "compound" of body and soul remains. Without it, we have entered a world of pure intellection which is not a human world at all.

The Meaning of Soul

The tension which arises from the ensouled body which is a human being has several significant consequences. First, with the possible exception of Aristotle's self-moving soul, the Greek concept of soul suggests that soul is more of a mechanism to attune humans to their world than to initiate their own activity. Soul's job is to provide a medium through which human responses to the external world are expressed, not to pull humans up by their bootstraps in order to ignore, surmount, or ultimately transcend their world. This puts a substantial premium on the human environment, which is the source of both what is useful and what is dangerous for humans. We have long been accustomed to the Christian view of a world created good by god, but turned toward evil by what lies within the human will. For the Greeks, however, the equation is reversed. For the Greeks, corruption and harm come from the outside, not the inside. Corruption and imperfection do not arise from some supposed intrinsic capacity or desire to do evil, but from forces outside that cause humans to do what is less – and often far less – than good.

From this it follows that summoning up "inner strength" is no way to defeat external corrupting forces. There is no hope down this course, because humans have no independent point from which to exercise leverage against the world. What is required to defeat, or at least to turn away, an external corrupting force is not inner strength or "will," but an even stronger force that can overpower it. The way to overcome the love of other human bodies is not to teach resistance to this love. So much the less is it to moralize about the consequences of this love. Rather, it is to instill an even more powerful kind of love which will supplant—by tempering, in this case—the love of specific bodies. As humans, we are moved by the love or desire which is implicit in our imperfection. The way to shape that love is to put in place a more powerful directive love which can provide deeper and more lasting, though never fully complete, satisfaction. In each case this directedness depends upon a lack, a need, a deficiency that characterizes human beings. Soul is an expression of the finitude implicit in *eros* or desire.

Here we find no psychology of human "freedom." Here we find no black box of the human ego which goes about acting as if the entire world were its raw material. Here we find no "breaking free" of external forces – whatever this might mean – in order to expand an imaginary internal realm of human freedom. The goal is rather to order one's actions according to the best external forces, that is, those which allow human soul to exercise its capabilities in the fullest possible way. This is why it is vitally important in the Greek world to monitor and to regulate closely what comes into and what acts through one's soul from the outside. Diet and air are the staples of the human environment. Regulating these fundamental intakes is the key to the health of the body. These must be carefully tended to produce health. And when health breaks down and illness occurs, Greek medicine responds in an appropriate way: the treatment of sickness consists invariably in some form of purging. Sickness is treated by lancing, by bleeding, or by sweating, each in the service of forcing, or at least allowing, what has come in from the outside to go back out once again.

Regulation is no less critical for the non-physical inputs of human life. It is vital to control and to shape the educational, familial, and cultural factors which constitute the environment of human soul. These external social inputs will shape the qualities of the human souls which operate within them. It is impossible to suppose that one can have a social order which values courage if courage is not taught, and taught unrelentingly, to young people. It is impossible to suppose that one can have a social order that values any other virtue if this virtue is not taught fulsomely and repetitively to young people whose souls are learning how to express and order themselves.

Each level of the social order plays a role in shaping the environment for human souls. But none plays a larger or more complete role than the political order. Here one finds an entity large enough and complex enough to give scope to the question of how best to live, that is, to the question of justice. Here is where the practices of families are encouraged or restrained; here is where the work of different classes of producers and consumers is regulated; here is where decisions are made about who are and who are not enemies of the political order, and about who will defend the order and in what ways. Here is the level at which the full panoply of questions about how social life is to be lived can and does find expression. All of this places the political order in a pivotal role in the encouragement of what soul will seek.

In this way, the question of a good political order is raised in a different manner than it is in the Torah. In the Torah the worship of Yahweh by the people of Israel is the beginning and end of wisdom, and the goodness of the tribe is judged by how well or poorly it is carrying out this task. The quality of the life of any individual is not a desideratum here. For the Greeks, however, there is an element – which should admittedly not be overstated – by which not only individuals are judged by their role in the political order, but by which the political order itself is judged in terms of accommodating the fullest possible ends of human soul. Living in a well-constructed social order is important both for the tribe of Israel and a member of a Greek polis. Some degree of tension between what is good and the tribal order of Israel is indeed possible. After all, kings of Israel might – and often did – deviate from the commands of Yahweh. To bring such rulers back to Yahweh is the aim and the burden of the Hebrew prophets. But when this occurs, and the tribe follows Yahweh's commands, that is all that can be said. It is not as if there is an external, or additional, standard by which the relative goodness of the tribe of Israel can be measured. It is not as if the independent human fulfillment of the lives of individual Hebrew tribal members offers any way to validate externally the goodness or lack of goodness of the tribe.

For the Greeks there is a fundamental tension that is missing in the Torah. Belonging to a well-ordered tribe (or polis) may be the beginning, but it is not the end of wisdom. Following the commands of Yahweh (or the gods of the polis) is not the way to live a fully good life. For the Greeks the answer is never quite so simple. One lives in a political order, as one must; it is the way humans live, and it will influence strongly the kinds of expression that one's soul will manifest. But the political order itself can and must be judged in some measure by how well it conduces to the fullest human possibilities, in a way which is simply absent from the teachings of Moses. This Greek view should not be misunderstood as a full-blown doctrine of the consent of the governed, by which the political order is judged only by how it satisfies the goals of its individual members. We moderns set up individuals as the arbiters of the political order, thus making the political order a very contingent entity. Our modern individualism somewhat depreciates the need for a good political order because it supposes that, after all, however bad the political order, we can maintain some independent stance against it. For the Greeks, opposition to the political order was a deeply serious matter; not every random view of each and every random Greek had the standing to judge the whole. But still and all, there remains a lasting tension between the life of the political order in which one lives, and one's life as an ensouled human. Such is the meaning and force of the concept of human soul.

This tension cannot be overcome or transcended in a lasting way. There is implicit in the Greek idea of soul a clear sense of human limitation. Humans neither can nor ever will be free of external influences; they can hope only to be shaped by the best of these influences, by the ones which allow us to express the fullness of our possibilities most reliably and consistently. So long as soul is embodied it will operate through the senses and the other physical characteristics of the body. There is no realistic chance that living human beings can ever become a lasting part of the One, the Good, or to become a god. Human soul is and will remain imperfectly able to overcome its human condition. Temporary and partial escape (*katharsis*) from the limitations of human life is indeed possible, but it will remain at best temporary and partial. A temporary glimpse of what transcends human limitation is possible, when one is moved partially beyond the immediacy of one's time and place and body. But whether this is called knowing the *Eidos* or a mystical union with the All, the One, or the Good, it is a deep but passing joy after which the finitude of human life soon reasserts itself.

The compound of soul and body which we are is thus always limited. There is no chance for humans to live fully and permanently at one with what is permanent, comprehensive and transcendent. Nor can any human being who aims best to fulfill his essence, that is, to express human soul most fully, find complete fulfillment in the specificity of his family, his friends and acquaintances, or his political order. It is the fate of the ensouled body which is the human being to be finite, limited and incomplete.

Yet for all of that, there is a deep liberation in the Greek idea of soul. The teachings of the Torah point beyond human life to Yahweh. But the human project there is not to *be* like Yahweh, but to obey his commands. This is a clear and unambiguous expression of human finitude and limitation. The Greek view of soul also expresses human finitude and limitation, but it points beyond that limitation. It points beyond finitude and toward the possibility that at least to a degree, one can be more like the One, the All, the Good, not just to worship it from afar. Yahweh offered a promised land which, though never reached in the Torah, was a plot of land for the tribe of Israel. The Greek concept of soul offers a kind of interior promised land in which humans can know what is their goal, even if they too will be frustrated in reaching that goal. The promised land of the Torah is mundane, physical and geographic. It is found in the Middle East. The promised land of the Greek soul is a glimpse of the One and some limited participation in it. This participation points one well beyond one's finite, sense-laden human life. It dissolves our particularity into the whole in a way which ultimately breaks down human individuality altogether. As Plato says in the *Phaedo,* "all souls are by nature equally souls." In overcoming our temporal, spatial, physical and political/tribal limitations, we move – fitfully and fleetingly during this life while we are ensouled – beyond the qualities we associate with everyday human life. This is how the essence of human being, namely soul, fulfills itself. In so doing, it both confirms and points beyond the limitations of human being.

THREE

EMBODIED WILL:

ON BEING CHRISTIAN

And the word became flesh....

John 1:14

EMBODIED WILL:

ON BEING CHRISTIAN

Christian faith has expressed itself in radically different ways throughout its two thousand year history. The life of a Christian martyr in the Colosseum; of an ascetic in the sands of the desert; of a crusading emperor; of an evangelical preacher; or of a professor of Christian theology—each such life, and many others as well, has given its expression of faith a unique accent and force. The experiential life of Christianity is wide indeed. What it means to be a Christian is thus not a question to be answered too quickly or too simply. This is all the more true as Christianity is not an ancient philosophy whose adherents have long since passed away, but a faith which continues to unfold as it encounters contemporary challenges.

Nevertheless, if there be such a thing as Christian faith, it must be possible to speak about what it is. What has been the fundamental teaching or doctrine of Christianity? What are its unique characteristics and contributions to the intellectual history of the West? And what is the distinctive Christian understanding of what it means to be human and of how human life is best fulfilled?

We begin with a brief comment on today's Christianity, lest we miss the mark altogether. Broadly speaking, contemporary Christianity sees itself as an antidote to an age of material self-indulgence. It is the exponent of matters of the spirit in a dispirited age; it is the defender of the soul in a soulless world of scientific and cultural materialism. It calls upon human beings to look to higher spiritual pursuits as against crass and excessive indulgence in physical, material pleasures. It upholds the spiritual dimension which calls humans out of the narrow, day-to-day concerns of their rootedness in time and space.

However true this may be (and we will consider in Chapter Five whether today's prevalent secular view is really materialistic at all), such a view misconstrues altogether the core teaching of Christianity and its distinctive contribution to Western thinking about what it means to be human.

We have already seen that the concept of soul was highly developed, particularly in Greek thinking, centuries before the advent of Christianity. These doctrines were widespread in Roman and Jewish thought by the time of Jesus. Jewish thinking had evolved considerably, especially in the thought of the Pharisees who were open to Greek philosophical ideas, from its earlier expression in the books of Moses. Though the idea of a non-material soul is taken over in early Christianity, it is done so without any significant emphasis. The concept of soul does not play a central role in the New Testament canon. Jesus scarcely refers to human soul at all, and when he does it is usually in the broadest sense of the word, meaning "life." The word "psuche" or its variant is found one hundred and four times in the New Testament, usually not in a technical sense but in a way better understood as "life" or "person." Acts 27:37, for example, reads that "we were in all in the ship two hundred and seventy-six souls." One would look in vain in the New Testament for a doctrine which abstracts and elevates "soul" as the cardinal teaching of what it means to be human.

Where the idea of human soul is later developed in the teachings of the church fathers including Augustine and Aquinas, to name two only, it is as a response to Greek doctrines rather than as a direct flowering from the text of scripture itself. Absent Greek philosophy, it would be impossible to infer the doctrine of soul which developed in historic church Christianity from the New Testament, much less from the words of Jesus.*

As a purely logical matter, it is possible to imagine the evolution of a Christian doctrine that maintained full consistency with the Greek view of soul. Upon such a view, soul would join body to animate human life until the union of soul and body is dissolved at death. Historic Christianity might then have held that the fate of soul at death depends upon faith in the truth of Jesus' claims. A believer's soul would be rewarded, an unbeliever's punished. All this would be largely congruent with the classical Greek view. To be sure, the classical Greek view would not have based the prospect of punishment or reward in the afterlife upon an attitude of faith concerning a specific set of claims; it would have based punishment or reward, if they were to occur at all in an afterlife, upon the quality of an entire human life and its actions. Nevertheless, such a view would have preserved in Christianity the standard Greek philosophical view of the departure of soul from body at death.

The Resurrection of the Body

But this is most decidedly *not* the direction which historic church Christianity takes. Christianity represents a radical turn from the Greek doctrine of soul. It also makes a radical departure from the teachings of the books of Moses, which are relatively silent about what occurs after death. The distinctive teaching of Christianity is to be found in the way in which it elevates the importance of body. This is reflected in the very

* John Paul II speaks to this in the encyclical "Fides et Ratio," where he accords philosophy a positive role in helping to understand and elaborate what is the faith of Christianity. In his lecture at the University of Regensburg entitled "Faith, Reason and the University," Pope Benedict XVI refers to the "inner rapprochement between Biblical faith and Greek philosophical inquiries" which he calls an event of decisive importance for world history.

idea of the in-carnation. In the incarnation God does not assume a human *form*, but becomes a human body, a living flesh and blood human being who hopes and fears and feels the pain of physical suffering. The most important ritual of the Christian faith, holy communion, describes the way in which humans are to share an intimate relationship with God. This is not a ceremony of intellectual reverie. The ritual of communion – of communing with, or being in intimate rapport with God – suggests a different route: one communes with God by eating the flesh and drinking the blood of God. The sheer physicality of the ceremony is difficult to miss. It is in this sense thoroughly un-Greek.

But Christian doctrine goes far beyond this point in elevating the importance of body. What, after all, is the cardinal tenet of Christian faith? What is the signal event which defines Christianity, which validates its truth, and without which its leading apostle has said that a Christian's faith is "futile" and his life is to be "pitied?" It is the resurrection of Jesus. Paul says at Corinthians I, 15:14: "...if Christ has not been raised, then our preaching is in vain and your faith is in vain." It is the resurrection not of Jesus' soul, but, as the creeds say, "of the body." The early church struggled long and hard to expunge any hint of a doctrine which spiritualized the meaning of the resurrection. The resurrection of Jesus was not to be understood metaphorically, or as a spiritual or psychic event. To the contrary, the resurrection of Jesus was the resurrection of his entire psychosomatic being. Not the resurrection of Jesus' soul, but the resurrection of Jesus whole. Indeed, at John 11:25 Jesus says flatly "I am the resurrection." The implications of this distinctive doctrine are far-reaching and go to the core of Christianity's contribution to understanding what it means to be human.

Why is the resurrection of the body so important in

Christianity? What does this mean? For it is not only Jesus' body that was resurrected. It is not even just the bodies of all believing Christians that are resurrected. Christian doctrine holds that there will be a resurrection of every human body which has ever lived. On this day of judgment all human bodies and souls will be reunited. This is a singularly Christian idea, not to be found in Greek or Hebrew predecessors.

In order to appreciate the singularity of this view, let us review the historic Christian church view of body and soul. Christianity shares the Greek view that each human being is en-souled body. Soul is what en-livens body, what enables and expresses human movement, growth and decay, sensation, perception, and thinking. Soul enables human beings to have a relationship with God. Soul is the medium through which God can and does work in human beings. Soul enables humans to do good and to do evil. Soul is the faculty which allows human beings to turn toward God or away from God. Soul is the instrument through which humans can be attuned generally, but most importantly either toward or away from God. It is a capacity which other animals and plants do not have. Human soul is what permits the full range of human choices and actions which make us human. In this regard, soul seems like it might be either a blessing or a curse. Plants and animals do not possess the range of capabilities which take them to the threshold issue of human existence: the ability to know God or to turn away from God. For humans alone the stakes are very high. Would it be preferable to be a human who is punished for all eternity than to be an animal which, while not possessing the chance to know God, at least is in no danger of eternal punishment? After all, Jesus said of Judas "It would be better for him if he had not been born" (Mark 14: 21).

Human soul permits humans to be oriented toward what is good or evil, toward or away from God. The phrase "the spirit is willing but the flesh is weak" is a peculiarly un-Christian phrase. It is through soul that all human action occurs. Human body is a necessary condition for sin to occur, but it is always through the instrument of soul that the body is moved to good or ill.

Where does soul "come from?" And at what point does soul enliven the material body to make it a human being? Little is said about this in the New Testament and it remained to work out an answer to this question in the first centuries after Jesus, as Christianity grappled with this and other questions put to it by Greek philosophical thinking. From the beginning, Christianity inclined toward the view that soul does not pre-exist the human body with which it joins. A pre-existent soul which floats about freely before attaching itself to a body would suggest the possibility of souls coming into and going out of bodies over time. These re-incarnated souls would in turn suggest that the death of Jesus did not atone once and for all for the sin of the whole human being. The idea of pre-existent soul (advanced by Origen) was anathematized at the Second Council of Constantinople in 553.

Soul itself then comes into being at the moment of its union with the physical human body. But where does soul come from? Here early Christian doctrine is less resolutely clear. One can find suggestions that soul is breathed into humans at birth by God, much like was supposed to have occurred when God "breathed" life into Adam. Others argued that ensoulment occurred through the natural process of conception and birth, though there was at that time limited knowledge about the science of conception. At the risk of overstatement, it would be fair to say that early church Christianity occupied itself far more fully with what happened to soul at death than with where, when, and how ensoulment first occurs. There are today, of course, more pressing reasons to put the question of ensoulment into the center of Christian reflection. Given modern medical capabilities to prevent conception and to destroy what is conceived, the question of en-soulment is more urgent. If en-souled being is human being, and if humans are en-souled at conception, then destroying what is conceived is destroying human life.

Each soul uniquely en-souls that body with which it is joined. This is nowhere plainly said in the Scripture, but is a broad inference from God's ensoulment of each and every human being. Given that soul is the medium through which humans are moved, it is difficult to say clearly how and in what ways this medium would differ from one human being to another. And if souls do so differ, it would seem God makes that difference to occur and that humans are thus rather fully determined by how God has ensouled them in the first place. This is perhaps another way of speaking of grace, which we will discuss shortly.

Just as in classical Greek thought, Christianity understands death to be the moment that body and soul separate from one another. A body without soul lacks all capability of self-movement, sensation, perception and thought. Without this power it is unable to replenish itself and undergoes a process of disintegration. It loses the power which holds it together, the power of soul. But if the body disintegrates at death, in Christian doctrine the soul "lives" on. To say it "lives" is of course problematical, for the very definition of life is en-souled body, and at death body is no longer present with soul—an argument made by Luther for the soul's mortality. Clearly, this "life" must be of a rather different sort than the bodily human life with which we are familiar. In fact, it is difficult to comprehend any idea of the subsequent life of soul without describing that life in a thoroughly metaphorical way, drawn analogously to physical life. Soul persists after death, but even to hint at how it persists seems to require a physical analogy of one kind or another.

What occurs to soul after death? What is this "life" like? At times it is said that post-death soul inhabits a "place." This might be heaven or hell, but in what sense this is a "place" – since soul is immaterial – is rather hard to say. This "place" might be imagined to be "above" or "below" the earth, again reflecting the fact that without analogy to the physical world little could be said about soul after death.

The souls of deceased humans are accorded differing fates, depending upon their human life on earth. Prior to Jesus' death, it seems that few souls were accorded a particularly joyful existence. In the Hebrew Bible only those with special qualities were said to be "with God" after death. In Christianity this abode of human soul is far more widely generalized. Jesus, for instance, tells the criminal on the cross next to him that on that very day he would be "with God."

Historic church Christianity held the notion that at the moment of death all souls "go somewhere." If souls are sorted out on the basis of faith, some will be rewarded and the rest punished. This is a rather bright line test – either to be eternally rewarded or eternally punished, with no middle ground. Should not the punishment fit the crime in a more discriminating and proportionate way than the either/or of salvation or damnation? This would certainly accord better with ordinary human notions of justice. This is all the more true, as humans seem to have better or worse chances in earthly life of becoming adherents to the one faith which will justify them. In this regard, there evolved in the church a doctrine of an inter-mediate fate for some souls – to be in purgatory rather than heaven or hell. Scriptural evidence for such a "place" is scanty at best, and Protestants have pointed out that the issue of whether Jesus did or did not fully atone for humans (or whether more than the sacrifice of the cross is required to achieve salvation) is at stake with this notion. The "all or nothing" judgment of God was certainly always understood as God's prerogative. And it was never to be doubted that God's wisdom and justice might well differ from human wisdom and justice. But still and all, church fathers created with the idea of purgatory a temporary alternative to the sheer either/or doctrine of heaven and hell.

How is soul described after death? Those souls which are rewarded, or saved, are said to be "with God." Such a description would permit of a less-than-fully physical analogy. Souls could be "with God" in the way a dream is present before a sleeper. One is experiencing in ways which seem very real, but the objects being experienced need not be physically present. This is a kind of non-physical experiencing. Souls are perhaps "with God" in some way not possible on earth. Souls could perhaps feel close to God without an actual physical closeness. "Sitting at the feet of god" would be understood entirely metaphorically.

And the souls which are punished? Today's Roman Catholic Catechism says that such souls suffer the absence of God. Why being absent from God should be more painful after death than it is for human beings who turn away from God during their earthly lives is not convincingly said. Indeed, a certain soft "correctness" has settled into the contemporary church. Early church doctrine followed more carefully Jesus' statement that the souls of the damned suffer in a lake of "fire." How bodiless souls can burn and suffer in fire became the object of a centuries-long interpretive quest. Moreover, since those in purgatory are said to be experiencing a "cleansing fire," one might ask why those who are damned should be experiencing a less frightful fate.

But for Christianity this is not the end of the story. And

herein lies the key aspect of what is unique and distinctive about Christian doctrine. At some future moment in historical time (often said to be "soon" in the New Testament) Jesus will return to earth and there will be a final judgment of all humans who are then living and all who have ever lived. At this time the souls of the dead will be reunited with their human, earthly bodies. This is not intended as a metaphor, but rather quite literally; each soul will reunite with the body of its earthly, human life.

This is pre-figured by what occurred at the death of Jesus. At Jesus' death his soul and body were separated and his body was placed in a tomb. Within three days his body and soul were reunited; Jesus was resurrected.* When Jesus reappears after his death, he is at times described in a somewhat ghost-like way, somewhat like the Greek shades in Hades. Standing outside the tomb, Jesus tells Mary not to hold on to him. But the Scripture makes clear that the resurrected Jesus walked, talked, ate, and retained the wound in his side – all of which could occur only in an actual physical human body. The resurrected Jesus tells his disciples: "See my hands and my feet, that it is I myself; touch me and see, for a spirit does not have flesh and bones as you see that I have" (Luke 24:39).

Jesus' resurrection is generalized in Christian doctrine to everyone, the living and the dead, believers and unbelievers alike. When Jesus "returns" to earth a second time, the souls and bodies of everyone will be reunited. Each soul will be matched again with its earthly body and with no other. How

---

* Debate in the early church occurred over whether Jesus' body decayed during its days in the tomb. The dominant view was that uniquely, Jesus' body did not decay before he was resurrected. This would suggest that some tangible atoms, those which comprised Jesus' body at death, are in some way divine. The Roman Catholic Church has held that Mary's body did not decay either. It is unclear why it is important to assert these doctrines, but they do reflect the powerful emphasis on physicality in the church.

can this be? The first and most important statement about the reunified body/soul is Paul's. At Corinthians I 15:35 ff, Paul says: "It is sown a physical body, it is raised a spiritual body. If there is a physical body, there is also a spiritual body." Leaving aside the rather doubtful logic of the second half of his formulation, what could this possibly mean? The phrase "spiritual body" is an oxymoron, like "round square." "Spiritual body" is not without clear meaning because it is difficult or laborious to form an image of it. Rather, everywhere the words "spirit" and "body" are used, they are meant to exclude one another. What is spirit is *not* body and what is body is *not* spirit. What could Paul mean to be doing in forcing these concepts together in a "spiritual body?" Some have said that it is a "mystery." But surely this response begs the question: why just this mystery, in just this way? Why is this particular mystery, rather than another, necessary to the doctrine at all?

What is so important about the physical bodily dimension of the resurrection – as opposed to the continuing persistence of soul alone after death? After all, Christianity seems to adopt the view of bodiless, free-floating souls for the period between human death and the final judgment. Here it seems that souls which are detached from body can somehow experience either joy or suffering. If soul can suffer in fire, or in cleansing fire, before the second coming, why is it necessary to have a body to suffer eternally? Why must humans suffer with their bodies, if evil spirits who have no body are said to suffer in eternal fire? Evil spirits – who never had, do not have, and never will have bodies – suffer the same fate in the lake of fire as do unbelieving humans with bodies.

Augustine spoke directly in his *City of God* (Book XXII, Chapter 29) when he said that he had no clear understanding of what eternal life will be like, for the simple reason that "it has

122 Against Modern Humanism

never come within the range of my bodily senses." Augustine here takes the quite reasonable view that sensible experience is that which is experienced by and in body. Without body there is no sensible experience. Thus, if we are to speak at all sensibly about life after death we must do so in physical terms. We must analogize what life without body is like – or we must assert the doctrine that life after death will again be with body. Christianity actually does both.

Augustine's caveat did not dissuade numerous Christian writers from long-running speculation and disputation about the character of life after death. Indeed, Augustine himself was not dissuaded. His careful statement above comes in the 29th of 30 chapters of just such extended speculation. What is the Scriptural warrant for elaborating what life is like after death? Jesus himself did not speak very much about it. He said essentially that believers will be with God and that non-believers will burn in the lake of fire. When confronted with the question of the man who married seven sisters, he suggested that there would be no institution of marriage in the afterlife. From this it could be inferred, as most subsequent thinkers did infer, that male and female would exist as separate genders in heaven. Beyond these few hints, Jesus did not describe life after death.

Elsewhere in the New Testament, however, there is no uncertainty whatever about the day of final judgment. On that day souls and bodies are reunited. They may be reunited as "spiritual bodies," as bodies which are "fleshless, bloodless bodies," as bodies which display a "one to one correspondence to human bodies," or according to any number of other metaphors. But bodies they are that unite with soul to re-establish the whole psychosomatic being which lived on earth. Indeed, the mainstream historical church argued that it is the precise, selfsame constituents of each person's earthly body that are reunited with soul. It did not matter that these bodies had long since disintegrated in their tombs; that they had been dismembered by wild animals; that they had been burned in the fires of martyrdom; or that they had been eaten by vultures (and thus again animated in these creatures).

Some Christians like Origen, who were more deeply influenced by Greek thinking, argued that the human body was a dynamic physical being, not always possessed of precisely the same atomic constituents at each point in its life. He no doubt had an instinct, but really no clear idea how true this is. But his point was that it does not matter whether the material parts of the human body come and go, for this is not the important aspect of what survives death. Soul should be our focus in the afterlife. For this and other like views, many of Origen's positions were later anathematized by the church.

The nature of post-earthly life was debated in excruciating detail in the early church. Which body is to be rejoined with soul at the time of final judgment? The body at the time of its earthly death? The middle-aged body? The adolescent body? Although far from dogmatic about it, Augustine supposes the body to be rejoined to soul would be the body at roughly thirty years of age. This is the age of the fully mature body and, parenthetically, roughly Jesus' age at the time of his ascension. Almost despite itself, this doctrine suggested the corollary that those who die as infants would receive their earthly bodies at the final judgment as they "would have become" when they reached the age of thirty years, an interesting departure from soul's reunion with its actual physical body.

Church fathers debated the question whether bodies would be raised with or without "blemish" or imperfection. Would the lame be raised so they could walk and the blind be raised with sight? Most argued that earthly imperfections would vanish, or at least be of no consequence. Some church fathers exempted from this the martyrs of the faith. Ordinary humans might be raised without the scars of their earthly suffering, but martyrs would bear the scars of their martyrdom as badges of honor at the final judgment.

Church fathers also debated how the more carnal earthly pleasures would be experienced in the afterlife. On the basis that Jesus ate and drank after his resurrection, most commentators argued that the reunited body/soul would enjoy food and drink, including wine. At Mark 14:25, Jesus says he will enjoy the fruit of the vine "anew in the kingdom of God." Church fathers argued that the saved would not eat from necessity, that is, from hunger – because that would suggest a deficiency in heaven – but only for enjoyment (not the counsel of nutritionists today, to be sure). And what of sex? As parts of the human body, sexual organs would no doubt be raised from the dead along with the rest of the human body. Would these organs be used by the reunited soul/body after the final judgment? As one might suppose, opinions varied here, especially since there would be no institution of marriage in heaven. Augustine argued that the resurrected world would not be a fallen world of sin; he had the considerable daring to argue that what is a sexual sin on earth would be no sin at all in heaven. After all, before the fall, Adam and Eve experienced no shame about sex.

In all of this, the place of the body displays itself in the center of Christian thinking. Surely God has the power and ability to reassemble the atoms of each earthly body and to re-join them with their unique human soul at the time of judgment. One would not have to deny God's power to do this in principle to wonder why he would do it in fact. Why should this be so critical to Christian doctrine? What is so important about the body? There is no doubt that the hope of the resurrection of the body offered considerable solace for the horrific martyrdoms in wave after wave of persecution before Christianity was finally adopted as an official religion by Constantine. We have seen many instances in history, including in our own time, of the power of the hope of resurrection to inspire human action, including suffering and death.

But it was not only against Roman persecution that the resurrection of the body played a critical role. During the early centuries of the church there was a deep doctrinal struggle over what would become the core of Christianity. There were constant pressures from those who wished to shape Christianity into a more spiritualized, more intellectual, more Greek teaching. These were the advocates of the doctrine of *gnosis*. Gnosis was by no means a doctrine which struggled against Christianity from the outside, as it were; gnosis aimed in many instances to *be* the authentic interpretation of Christianity itself. In speaking about competing currents of religious thought, a leading interpreter of gnosticism, Kurt Rudolph aptly says that a separation of "orthodoxy" and "heresy" is inappropriate for the first two centuries after Jesus.

There is much in the core teachings of the New Testament canon which is difficult to square with gnostic doctrine. But we should recall that there was no accepted New Testament canon – or even an accepted Old Testament canon – in the early years after Jesus. Marcion, for example, taught that the Hebrew Bible, with its imperfect and despicable gods, was the very antithesis of the god of Jesus. Lest we dismiss Marcion as a poor Christian, or as no Christian at all, he was the first Christian to draw up a New Testament canon. Gnostic teachings were a powerful stimulus, if not the chief stimulus, to the creation of a thoroughly developed Christian theological doctrine. The author of the full-blown Christian ecclesiastical system, Irenaeus, developed his thinking about the church as a specific response to gnostic teachings.

Gnostic doctrine taught that the body, and indeed all of physical creation, is corrupt. The material world is so corrupt that a good god could not possibly have created it; the earth and all of its inhabitants must have been the creation of a lower or lesser god.* For a gnostic the last thing that would be desirable is the resurrection of the body, whether a "spiritual body" or a body of any other kind. The goal of gnosis is escape from the body. Salvation is achieved when one's true interior self can at last be free from the corruption of the body, with all of its hindrances, limitations, decay and finitude.

The Hebrew Bible, on the other hand, from the very beginning sees the creation as good. This affirmation of the physical world continues throughout the New Testament, including the incarnation, communion, resurrection, and the final judgment. It is the thrust of historic church Christianity to defend the physicality of the created world as a positive act of God. In Rudolph's words, historic Christianity aims to rehabilitate the created world from the negative position of its demiurgical origin. The world of creation is not evil by nature, nor are the bodies that inhabit it. Christian teaching affirms the goodness of creation and body. In commenting on Buddhism's view of the world in *Crossing the Threshold of Hope*, for example, John Paul II notes critically:

> To liberate oneself from [this] evil, one must free oneself from this world, necessitating a break with the ties that join us to external reality – ties existing in our human nature, in our psyches, in our bodies. The more we are

---

* Here gnostic doctrines leaned on Plato's story in the *Timaeus* that the cosmos is the creation of a god who is not so perfect as to be content simply to be in his own being. This less perfect god is often called a "demiurge."

> liberated from these ties, the more we become
> indifferent to what is in the world…

He might also have been speaking about gnosticism or of any other idealism. For Christians no such liberation is possible. Nor is liberation from the body desirable. For at bottom Christianity defends the notion that without body there is no full meaning to joy or to suffering. Christianity does not countenance complete joy or suffering in a non-bodily way. It rejects the abstruse philosophical doctrine of a bodiless soul in favor of what is tangible, real and human. In that interim period between death and the final judgment, soul is given body-like characteristics which will become, it seems, richer and fuller on the day of final judgment. We should not say that for Christians the fate of the saved is "like" joy. The fate of the saved *is* joy, though perhaps hard for us to comprehend. And the fate of the damned is not "like" torment; it *is* torment, though also hard to comprehend. The suffering of the damned is real, physical torment. At times this torment is taken to great heights, even suggesting at Revelation 14:10 that the followers of the beast will be tormented "in the presence of the holy angels and the Lamb." Presumably this intensifies the suffering of the damned as well as providing pleasure for the saved. John 6:10 says, after all, that the souls of martyrs seek revenge in heaven upon their earthly tormenters.

Augustine, who as always has a deep insight, moderates the notion of revenge in the afterlife. He argues that the blessed soul in the afterworld will have an intellectual, though not a sensible, recollection of earthly tormenters. The blessed soul will also be aware, as an intellectual matter, that the damned are suffering eternally. The blessed soul is aware of the suffering of the damned, but is not moved by it and does not derive pleasure from it. For Augustine – unlike the author of Revelation (and what thoughtful Christian has not at times shared Luther's wish that Revelation had been omitted from the canon?) – knowledge of misery seems to be an epistemological requirement of blessedness. If as Augustine says in *The City of God* (Book XXII), the blessed did not know misery, how could they sing the mercies of God? How could we experience joy if we did not know suffering? And how could the damned experience suffering if they did not somehow know joy? In Christianity joy and suffering are experienced sensibly, through the body—and not just any body, but the body of one's earthly life. Nowhere is this better expressed than in the pointed statement of Saint Jerome: "for it cannot be possible to sin in one body and be punished in another."

Christianity offers no abstract philosophical system, with an afterlife of contemplation of ideas or of immersion in the One or All. It offers an afterworld of physicality, a world that can thus be envisioned to some degree, and a world where joys and blessings are powerful enough to shape human behavior on earth. It would be difficult to imagine a view which ascribes to body more importance than does Christianity. Each human being is fated to be with his body forever and ever. Even atheistic materialism accords body only a temporary importance, that is, during one's earthly life. Freedom from one's body is simply not a consideration for Christianity; humans are fated to be with their bodies for all eternity.

This sets the stakes for earthly life extremely high. Perhaps the doctrine of repeated re-incarnation on earth seems harsh. Here souls must repeat life over and over again, sometimes in higher and sometimes in lower physical bodies, until soul learns its proper lesson and can achieve release. This is child's play compared with Christianity. In Christianity there is precisely one chance, precisely one finite human life, to make the correct choice – and upon that choice depends the eternal fate of one's entire psychosomatic being.

Salvation and Will

Given that humans are fated always to remain with their bodies in some way(s), how are they to ensure that their fate is a happy one? For there is no escape, no migration of soul, no complete forgetfulness to which to look forward. There is no way to relieve the condition of being body and thus of experiencing joy and suffering. The central practical question of Christian life is simply stated: how are we to be saved? How are we to achieve a life of eternal joy rather than eternal torment?

To the extent that either Hebrew thought or Greek thought spoke of an afterlife, it argued that a happy afterlife depends upon the quality of one's earthly life. But the quality of one's earthly life was normally measured by the accomplishment of great deeds. Christianity diverges radically from this path. In the place of great deeds, or works, is set the standard of faith. Great deeds cannot achieve for human beings a life of eternal joy; great deeds cannot achieve salvation. There is, to be sure, a different emphasis on the issue of deeds, or works, between historic church teaching and the later doctrines of Protestant Christianity. But this is a difference in accent and not of essence. For no Christian holds that salvation can be achieved through deeds, no matter how great, if faith is absent. What is required for salvation is faith – faith in the truth of scripture (and its elaboration through church tradition in the Roman Catholic Church). Good deeds or works may follow more or less inevitably from faith in the truth of scripture; but it is this faith which is the key to salvation. Faith is assent to or agreement with the teaching of Scripture. But what is faith and how does one come to possess it? What is the nature of the assent which is faith?

We might say first that Christian faith is not equivalent to human reason or thinking. The ability to think or reason makes faith possible, but it is not the cause of faith. Human reasoning is a necessary, but by no means sufficient condition of Christian faith. For a Christian cannot possibly reason his or her way to God. Christianity builds upon the fundamental unknowability of God in the Hebrew Bible. As we have said, the work of the god of the Hebrew Bible lies all about, but one cannot learn much of anything about that god from the external world. Virtually everything important about the Hebrew god is learned from the Hebrew Bible itself, including the laws, the rituals and the duties of human life.

Christianity follows this same course. One could study the external world forever and one would never infer from it that Jesus was the son of God, that he was physically resurrected, or that salvation and damnation are offered on a day of final judgment. For this one must turn to revelation, as it is unfolded in Scripture. One could arguably claim based upon reason alone that what exists must have had a creator, and one could call this creator Yahweh, God, or Allah. But to connect this bare conclusion with the specific revelations vouchsafed in any scriptural text requires a long step beyond human reason or thinking. It requires faith, or assent, to the truths of revelation on some basis apart from or beyond human thinking.

There is a very deep and thoughtful strain of Christianity, perhaps expressed best by John Paul II and Benedict XVI, which aims to establish the harmony of reason and faith. Benedict XVI says in his lecture "Faith, Reason and the University" that:

> biblical faith, in the Hellenistic period, encountered the best of Greek thought at a deep level, resulting in a mutual enrichment evident especially in the later wisdom literature. Today we know that the Greek translation of the Old Testament produced at Alexandria - the

> Septuagint - is more than a simple (and in that
> sense really less than satisfactory) translation of
> the Hebrew text; it is an independent textual
> witness and a distinct and important step in the
> history of revelation, one which brought about
> this encounter in a way that was decisive for the
> birth and spread of Christianity.

Upon this view we can say that God acts consistently with logos, and to do otherwise would be contrary to his nature. Reason and faith thus travel along the same path together, mutually reinforcing one another – at least as far as reason is able to travel.

But even this most philosophical strain of Christianity is clear that faith must take us beyond reason. Benedict XVI goes on to quote Paul approvingly when he says that love transcends knowledge and is "thereby capable of perceiving more than thought alone (cf. Eph. 3:19)." And other strains of Christianity are every bit as explicit as the Hebrew Bible in suggesting clear limitations on human thinking. The assent which is faith is not based upon complex thinking, much less upon a gnostic discipline of thought which is available only to a privileged few. The possibility of faith is offered democratically and quite liberally. This is aptly summarized at Matthew 7:7: "Ask, and it will be given you; seek, and you will find; knock, and it will be opened for you." Indeed, and again consistent with the thrust of the Hebrew Bible, human reason can even be a snare or a delusion which stands in the way of salvation. Jesus says at Matthew 11:25 (and Luke 10:21): "I thank you, Father, Lord of Heaven and earth, that you have hidden these things from the wise and understanding and revealed them to babes." This theme is taken up by Paul at Corinthians I, 1:2 (and Ephesians 3:19 and 4:17) who says that "the world did not know God through wisdom" and that "it pleased God through the folly of what we preach to save those who believe." In staking out a sharp distinction between Christianity and the claims of gnosis, Irenaeus says in *Against Heresies*:

> It is better if man knows nothing and does not perceive a single cause of things created but abides in faith in God and in love, rather than that, puffed up by such knowledge, he falls away from the love that makes man alive...and rather than that he falls into godlessness through the subtleties of his questioning and through hair-splitting.

Distinguishing himself from philosophers, or lovers of wisdom, most pointedly, Tertullian labels the "thirst for knowledge" a human vice. Augustine (*The City of God*, Book XIX) says: "...owing to the liability of the human mind to fall into mistakes, this very pursuit of knowledge may be a snare to him unless he has a divine Master, whom he may obey without misgiving..." And that excellent student of Augustine, Martin Luther – who aimed to simplify Christ's teachings – expresses it in his typically blunt Teutonic way when he says that "reason is the devil's whore."

If not by thinking or reason, how then is faith attained? At its core, faith is assent, faith is obedience, faith is submission. The Catechism of the Catholic Church says "By faith, man completely submits his intellect and his will to God." By what faculty does a human being submit his entire being to God? The answer to this lies in the future tense (English) verb which is hypostasized into the essential defining character of human soul: will. As a future tense verb, "will" implies a deficiency, a lack, a dissatisfaction with resting permanently in what is. It implies a making of things to change or to be different. Human soul enables for humans the full range of human expression, including motion, growth and decay, sensing, perceiving and thinking. But at the crown of human soul is will. Surely, intellect is a necessary condition of will; a plant does not "will" to move toward sunlight, nor an animal to hibernate. Thinking presents a human being with the ability to discern and discriminate; it is the groundwork for choosing. Without the fullness of human intellect, no willing is conceivable. But the intellect does not and ought not rule the Christian soul. What is the glory – or the downfall – of human soul is the power to choose which is called "will." Pope Gregory asserts in his *Letters*: "this is what it is to be human…a creature with a will." For a Greek philosopher, a human being is a thinking animal, a soul which finds its essential being in thinking. For a Christian, a human being is a willing animal, an embodied soul which finds its essence in choosing God.

At Matthew 15:10 ff Jesus speaks a revolutionary idea. He says: "Hear and understand: not what goes into the mouth defiles a man, but what comes out of the mouth, that defiles a man." Here is a view which the disciples said "offended" the Pharisees, and with good reason. But it was also one of those occasions when the disciples did not understand what they were hearing. Peter asks for an explanation and Jesus says:

> Whatever goes into the mouth passes into the stomach, and so passes on. But what comes out of the mouth proceeds from the heart, and this defiles a man. For out of the heart come evil thoughts, murder, adultery, fornication, theft, false witness, slander. These are what defile a man; but to eat with unwashed hands does not defile a man.

This is not merely a rejection of the rules of the Pharisees, or even of the priestly regulations of the Hebrew Bible. For the entire weight of all that had gone before – including both the Hebrew tradition and the Greek philosophical tradition – was that what goes "in" to a human is critical because this is what shapes human action. This is why eating, drinking and sex, not to mention art, music and poetry, must be so carefully regulated. Jesus turns this upside down. He suggests that within human beings there is internal latitude to shape ourselves. There are at least some actions which come "out of the heart" of humans, rather than from the external world. Humans seem to possess some degree of "freedom." As the un-coerced motion of soul, will is the distinctive human characteristic. Here is the true distinction between humans and animals. As possessors of instrumental reason there is only a quantitative difference between man and beast. As the being which is embodied will, humans are uniquely eternal creatures.

Human will may incline toward God or not. The will which turns toward God is good. It is good not because it is directed by intellect, but by its very choice of God. An evil will is one that turns away from God. There is no external cause of an evil act of will; it is determined within itself. Jesus suggests as much in his discussion of what defiles a human being. Every example he gives of what comes directly from within the human will is a negative, sinful one – murder, adultery, false witness and so forth. We will discuss the cause of good will soon. But here we should note that all that is evil comes from within the human being. The revolutionary grant of freedom for humans seems to be largely a license to sin.

This solves the theological problem of the origin of sin. God has created a good world. This world of materiality and of finitude is not, as the gnostics would have it, inherently evil or corrupt. Yet evil and corruption are all about. Where does evil come from? The origin of evil lies not in the world of God's creation, but in the latitude of humans to choose to turn away from God. This is well summarized by Augustine's mentor, Ambrose of Milan, who firmly rejects the Greek notion of danger and corruption coming into humans from the outside. Ambrose says in his *Exposition*:

> Greater danger lies not in attacks from outside, but from within ourselves. Inside us is the adversary, inside is the author of error, inside us I say, closed up within our very selves…it proceeds not from nature but from our own wills.

This act of volition or will is at once the distinctively human act and at the same time the source of evil in the world.

Will and Grace

If the choice to turn away from God rests squarely with the human being – whose will is thus the source of evil – the question of how and why a human turns toward God is more difficult. Jesus describes turning toward God as being born again: "I tell you the truth, no one can see the kingdom of God unless he is born again" (John 3:3). No human being had a choice about being born in the first place; one finds oneself put into the world whether one likes it or not. How is it possible for a human to be "born again?" Is this re-birth an act of un-coerced will? Is this an act of complete volition, of free and uncoerced choice? This turns out to be no easy question. For the death of Jesus on the cross was an atonement for human beings, and if humans are able to "earn" their salvation by turning freely toward God, this doubtless diminishes the importance of the gift of Jesus' sacrifice. If humans are good enough to be able to accept God through their own volition, why was this sacrifice necessary at all?

To answer these questions we must consider again the question of how humans are moved to choose. For although Jesus has accorded humans some ability to act out of their own being, particularly to choose evil, human activity is still rooted in a larger field of forces which moves humans to and fro. This is the world of spirits. Christianity holds the world to be populated by a multitude of spirits. These spirits, on analogy to the wind, are invisible forces which move the material world. One never sees the wind, but only its effects. One feels the power of the wind.

God himself is spirit. Though God can become material, as in the incarnation, God is understood as essentially spirit. Spirit is that which is not body, not confined to place and time. Spirit is abstract power, efficacy, capability, creativity. God as spirit cannot be known directly, but only through the ways in which he deigns to reveal himself so that finite humans can fathom something about him. He is said to "speak," to be "jealous," and to act through a host of other anthropomorphisms. He offers his "son" as a sacrifice so that humans can know about him. He inspires the text of scripture so there is a reliable account of him and of what humans ought to do to worship him.

There are also lesser spirits, spirits with more limited power, that have been created by God. These are called angels and demons. These may be pictured, or imagined, as having "ethereal" bodies which confine them less closely than humans to time and place. But these are just pictures. Angels and demons are bodiless spirits, or forces, which are able to move bodily beings by their power. As the Catechism says of angels: spirit is their nature, angel is their office. These lesser spirits and demons have the power to move human beings. They can also move what is not human. After all, when Jesus cast out a demon, he placed it into a herd of pigs that ran off a cliff. This was a matter about which neither the demon nor the pigs had a choice.

Spirit is no part of the make-up of a human being. Humans can be moved by spirit, but they are not themselves comprised in any part by spirit. Spirits may "dwell" in human beings, but they are not human at all. Paul says, for example, at Romans 8:9 that "the spirit of God really dwells in you." This spirit remains the spirit of God and not that of the human in which it dwells. Though it seems strange to say, in Christian doctrine human beings are not spiritual beings. To speak of "soul" and "spirit" interchangeably is easy enough – but it is to misunderstand the crux of centuries of debate about what would constitute Christian teaching. The gnostic view held that humans are comprised of three parts or aspects – body, soul, and spirit. For the gnostics, spirit is the most important, the essential quality of human being; spirit is the god-like part. The implication is clear: for the gnostics man is part god or part divine. The task of life is to free the divine part of man and to re-join it to the divine whole from which it has been broken off by its association with corrupt body.

Though spirit is mentioned in several places in the gospels, Christianity broadly rejects the view of humans as spirit. Humans are categorically not god-like. Humans may be created in God's "image." But whatever that might mean, it assuredly does not mean that humans are in any way gods. Humans can never cross the abyss which separates them from God. Even the saved in heaven, possessed of those fantastic "spiritual bodies," will be no part of God. They are said to "know" God or to "be with" God – but they are not god-like, much less a part of God.

Humans are not spiritual beings, but they can be and often are moved about by spirits. Spirits move humans by flooding into human soul, by infusing human soul, by influencing human soul. Human soul is moved by spirits, for good or ill, but does not itself become spiritual. Humans are always and everywhere comprised of soul and body only. Spirits come and go as they influence human soul, but do not become a "part" of the human being. That is why humans can have demonic spirits driven out of them, or exorcised. Their essential humanity is in no way changed by the act of exorcism; they have simply been liberated from an external force which has temporarily overwhelmed them.

The New Testament refers to a specific kind of spirit which it calls "holy." This is *pneuma hagios*, the spirit which is holy, the holy spirit. This spirit, this force, is a spirit sent by God himself. Indeed, this spirit seems to be a part of God himself. God is a spiritual being, despite the appellation of "father," and the holy spirit might be supposed to be the force of God himself entering into and infusing human soul. Much debate has ensued in the twenty centuries of Christianity about how to describe this force of God. The official view came to be that this spirit or force is a "person," though how this description illuminates the words of the New Testament is hard to say. It is understandable to seek an "image" of holy spirit, but spirit it remains for all of that. The holy spirit is perhaps best comprehended as God-in-action, God not in his role as lord of the universe, but God taking an active interest in specific humans and flooding his spirit through them. When Jesus said he would send a holy spirit to guide humanity, he seemed to mean that God would not leave people wholly to their own devices (and thus to choose evil), but would through this counselor or this spirit infuse and inform their lives.

To think of a triune God would be somewhat akin to thinking of a diune Satan. If Satan infuses a human soul with evil, is "all" of Satan dwelling in this soul? Or does some of Satan remain separate? Is not Satan exercising his power in the act of infusing a human soul? Is this not simply Satan-in-action? Or are we to suppose that Satan, who is already spirit, sends a separate person/spirit to do this work?

Whatever one makes of this arcane debate, it is evident that way; it merely seeks to extend whatever is human life forever.

Nor does the concept of ego speak accurately to what it means to be a human being. We are indeed fuller beings than can be described by how we are at any given moment. We receive hints about this all around us. But that our being is fuller than is expressed at any given moment certainly does not entail the notion that behind all this we are somehow an ego that lies beyond each and every one of our choices. Ego remains always beyond all of its choices, and beyond the entirety of the external world. The real and genuine freedom to be influenced by what is outside of ourselves is given away in favor of an illusory internal free ego that cannot be touched by the external world. To locate the fullness of being human, the relatively broad openness of human beings, in a fictional ego which lies at the center of all that is, ultimately destroys the actual fullness and the actual relative freedom of human beings. That we are somehow more than we are at any given moment does not entail the idea that we are therefore somehow infinite, pure or unfettered potential, that we are pure freedom. This is the long and unjustified inference that lies at the heart of contemporary egoism.

It is ironic that the ego which allegedly lies behind us is in fact destructive of genuine human individuality. When abstracted from all its externalizations this ego shrinks to a dot. The more ego is said to create, the less ego is. The fully self-created man would indeed be an impressive being – if only one could find the ego that is allegedly doing this creating. Once again we might let Goethe speak to the heart of the matter. In an arresting phrase in which he evaluates his merits as a writer and artist, he says "I did not make myself." There is no self-creating ego which lies behind the production of Goethe, which ego is somehow responsible for all he was and did. To assume so is simply to set up an abstracted essence to worship. It is to become fixed upon an illusory originator which, in fact, denies the fullness of human being.

Far better to preserve an openness to the possibility that we can genuinely learn from what is outside us, that we can genuinely transcend – at least to a degree – our own situation, by seeing it *as* our situation. The truly open way to live is to live as a being with multifold relationships with the external world. It is to live so as to be open to the possibility of learning from the world in all of its fullness – from nature, from our social world, and perhaps even from the gods. This is the truly human way to live.

When we live like this, we are likely to do so with a well-developed sense of humor. At the root of all humor lies both genuine knowledge and human finitude; we are striving to be more than we are, but we are still who we are. There is not much humor among the enforcers of the commands of a transcendent god. But there is equally little humor found among those for whom freely creating ego makes the entire world possible. These authors of immanent perfectionism cannot find humor or amusement in human finitude, or in any limits to their capacity to reshape the entire world. For them human finitude is a reproach, an alienated misunderstanding of our true power. A sense of humor derives from our genuine and curious human predicament, namely, that we can at once know beyond ourselves all the while we remain tethered to our time, place, gender, family, ethnicity, and nation and their various practices and foibles. People lack a sense of humor because they do not understand the world and the human place within it.

When we live like this, we will also cease to demand the plethora of "rights" and entitlements which characterize the contemporary world. If we have created ourselves, our lives are ours by right. If we truly have a "right" to everything, it is not surprising that we will live a life demanding our rights. We need not trouble ourselves about any sense of duty to others – which after all would reflect our finitude, our station in life, and our human limitations. We need only perpetually demand our rights and to live however we happen to please – for to whom or what in the external world could ego owe anything? If, however, we do not see ourselves as the creators or authors of our own lives, our sense of entitlement will shrink to reasonable bounds. This is the import of the Psalm that has come to be known as the Jubilate Deo: "Be ye certain that the Lord he is God; it is He that hath made us, and not we ourselves…" What could a fully self-made man owe to anyone else?

Howsoever we have come to be here, it is a gift and not a self-creation. It is enough to see a glimmer of immortality in which the particular is transformed within us – but we must accept our finitude as well. Our finitude draws us back perpetually into the world. Denying (rather than accepting) that finitude is the sham and hollow offer of contemporary egoism. Egoism destroys the basis of true openness which has always characterized the most fully human way to live. It is no shame to be a finite being, if we are striving against that finitude. This is consolation enough for our finitude. We cannot leap over or out of our limitations by creating an imaginary ego which lies behind and beyond all limitations. This ego is a myth, but unlike many other myths which at least point somewhere, it is peculiarly empty and destructive. It is destructive of the only humanity which is available to us. It is destructive of genuine self-knowledge and of the proper response to self-knowledge, which is gratitude for what there is. Yes, we strive against our limits. But as we do, it is enough to live gratefully in the world which we have been given.

throughout everything man remains man and God remains God. Adam is "psychic" and Jesus is "pneumatic" (Corinthians I, 15:44-46). Humans may be infused with the holy spirit or with an evil spirit. But humans do not become God or the devil; they act out the force of these spirits, but do not turn into these spirits. They remain human beings.

We can now return to our question. If humans are filled up and moved about by these spirits, can humans truly be said to be free? Can they exercise their wills in an uncoerced way? It is said in scripture that on one occasion God "deluded" certain people. How could a human being have the power to be free against God's overwhelming power to delude him? One has a sense from all this that humans may be filled up with holy or evil spirits from time to time, but perhaps on many occasions they are more or less left alone. When an evil spirit infuses a human soul, perhaps a human cannot resist it. Perhaps the only way to resist it is to be filled up with a more powerful spirit, a holy spirit – the power of God himself. When a human soul is filled up with a holy spirit, the most powerful spirit of all, God himself, there would seem to be little a human being could do to resist, if for some reason he wished to do so. Humans would seem to be powerless against God-in-action. God would shape their will entirely, and "will" would lose its ordinary meaning in such an instance.

There has been a broad range of views in Christianity about the latitude which God has accorded to humans to exercise their will to turn toward God. At one pole God's grace consists in the gift of his doctrine alone, and it is each human being's responsibility to accept that gift or not. Each human being is free to do so or not, and each human being will thus merit his reward or punishment. At the other pole is the sheerest predestination, in which God has determined from the beginning, as it were, who will be saved and who will be damned. Where is merit and

justice here? God's justice consists in this – every human being merits damnation. His mercy consists in this – that he should choose to save anyone at all.

Mainstream Christianity has opted for a middle position, without however denying the essential truth of predestination. The Catholic Catechism approvingly quotes Aquinas' form-ulation of how human beings come to faith: "Believing is an act of the intellect assenting to the divine truth by command of the will moved by God through grace." This formulation preserves, or at least aims to preserve, the "command" of human will, yet for all that, human will is moved by God. God's grace is here extended beyond the Pelagian notion that grace consists only in making the truth available, to be chosen or not. God's grace here is more active, moving and shaping the human will. With this we are nearly parallel with the characteristic Greek view, that humans act always according to the good, so far as they are given to know it. God's grace is the revelation of himself, which humans then choose to "will" as they are given it.

The fullness of human volition in Christianity thus remains somewhat ambiguous. But there is at least this much volition ascribed to humans – they are to remain open to receive the holy spirit. Humans can be turned rigidly against the holy spirit. In such cases God can still break through, even to a will deliberately turned against him if he wishes, of course – but, as in the case of Paul on the road to Damascus it is likely to be a violent and wrenching experience. Beyond this, who can say why or to whom God chooses to reveal his goodness, or to dispense his grace with irresistible force – or from whom he will withhold it altogether? We are lost again in mysteries which pass all human understanding.

Knowledge or intellection will not take us to the Christian God. One must set aside the quest to know God and instead

choose God. Perhaps this choosing will be described as fully free, perhaps as fully determined, or perhaps as the openness of one's will to be moved by God. One's intellect makes this choosing possible for humans in a way that is not possible for any other creature. But the crown of human soul is human will, the assent to or denial of God. One can hope – but never know for sure while one lives – that this assent is founded upon a gift of God and not upon a snare of delusion.

Individualism

Believing Christians are called on to be a part of the church, the body of Christ. Through membership in the church each Christian receives support and encouragement for his faith. Through the church Christians are called upon to extend that support and encouragement to others who are outside the church. It is not impossible to be a Christian living a solitary existence in the desert or the forest, but it is much more difficult. Communion with others in the church offers a way in which to make one's faith alive in the world, as opposed to a matter of private conviction.

For all of that, however, it is each individual Christian who will ultimately be judged. Each individual will be judged on his or her own, and not as a member of the faith, or the group, or the tribe to which one belongs. The eternal fate of the community is not at stake on the day of judgment; what is at stake is the fate of each human being as a discrete individual. This individual will persevere as the selfsame individual forever. Whether saved or damned, the unique ensouled human body which is each human being will carry forward in perpetuity.

There remains in Christian thought the interesting and somewhat anomalous period between the death of each human individual and the day of final judgment when Christ is said to return. During this period, which has now gone on for some

people for many thousands of years, soul and body are not quite united in the way they will be united upon Christ's return. During this time – which may be brief when measured in the grand scheme of things – souls seem to be embodied in a less than full way than will occur at Christ's return. Augustine says in *The City of God* (Book XIII) that "though there can be no manner of doubt that the souls of the just and holy dead live in peaceful rest, yet so much better would it be for them to be alive in healthy, well-conditioned bodies." For Augustine, and for Christian thinkers generally, there is no doubt about the inferiority of the free-floating, untethered soul to the soul which is rejoined to its earthly body. For life to be truly real, it must be sensible bodily life, not the pale immaterial shadowy life of souls moving about the ether of Hades. St. Bernard echoed this thought with the claim that he saw no way that happiness was genuinely possible in heaven until souls had once again been embodied. The continuing existence of a disembodied soul simply does not permit of a meaningful Christian afterlife. A meaningful afterlife demands resurrection of the body. And not just any body, but the very same body which was ensouled on earth. In his *Against John of Jerusalem,* St. Jerome speaks forcefully to this when he says of Job:

> ...if he is not to rise in his own sex and with the same members that were thrown on the dung heap, if the same eyes are not opened for seeing God by which they saw worms, where therefore will Job be? You [Origen] take away the things in which Job consists and give me empty words concerning resurrection.

Augustine ironically calls the day of final judgment the day of "second death." It is surely death in the sense that it is the final confirmation of the life of the damned forever. But it is no death at all in the ordinary sense of the word. Death means the

departure of soul from body on earth, the separation of soul and body. At the day of final judgment, soul and body are rejoined, not separated, and the second death is in fact the beginning of eternal life. On this day, one supposes that history as we have known it will end. There will be no wars or famines or crises which comprise so many of the events of human history. Yet in as much as the blessed are eating, drinking, and otherwise enjoying some version of bodily pleasure, human beings remain in some kind of time, not outside of time altogether. And in as much as the damned are experiencing some version of bodily suffering, they too seem to exist within time, if not within human history as we know it. Humans will never escape entirely from time; eternity is not outside of time, but is rather a very long time indeed.

All this takes us very far from Yahweh, who would punish the third, fourth and tenth generations for the sins of the first. For Christians, punishment is meted out to the very selfsame psychosomatic being who lived on earth and who perseveres as an ensouled body in the afterlife. The earthly sufferings of those who are good is of course as problematical for Christians as for anyone else, and are understood in the usual ways. Earthly suffering is a way God speaks to humans, and it is ultimately beyond human comprehension why it comes when and where and how it does. But for a Christian it is simply not comprehensible that God would allow a person to sin in one body and to be punished in another. At times Christians are tempted to think that when harm befalls sinners on earth, they are getting what they having coming to them. But it is no part of the doctrine that harm will befall some perpetually because of the sins of others. To the contrary, reward and punishment is meted out for all eternity directly to the innocent and guilty in their uniquely persisting ensouled bodies. There is a broad spectrum of Christianity from Pelagianism to predestination;

but wherever on this spectrum a Christian might fall, there is fundamental agreement on one principle. That principle is that God does not reward and punish others for the sins of some. He does not punish children for the sins of the fathers. God rewards and punishes each human being in his or her own skin, as it were. What is at stake in human life is the eternal fate of each unique, individual psychosomatic being.

Christianity defends the radicalism of this view against its principal opponents who would seek to loosen the permanent tie between body and soul. As we have discussed, the principal view against which historic church Christianity set itself was gnosticism, in all its variations. Any notion of souls and bodies casually mating, each to go its own way at death, was read out of the church as heresy. And it was not only in the early centuries of the church that gnostic strains arose. They have emerged from time to time throughout the history of the West, each time being met by forceful opposition. From time to time popular fairy tales or legends emerged which spoke of shape-shifting, or the power of soul to migrate from one kind of creature to another. These were strongly opposed by Christian doctrine, which saw in them an assault on the resurrection of the entire psychosomatic being. Human soul is different than what animates plant and animal bodies and it cannot inhabit their bodies. Indeed, one human soul cannot, does not and will not inhabit another human body either. Christianity remains insistent on the claim that each human soul will experience a reunion with the precise body it ensouled during earthly life.

Christianity also defended its claims against a cyclical view of human life and history. This cyclical view is not much in evidence today, having been thoroughly expunged (by Christianity) from the mind of the West, but it was far more prevalent in the years of the early church. On this view humans were condemned to repeat the cycle of birth, life, and death

endlessly. The history of the world was not linear, but circular, each event occurring again and again. But if each individual is a prototype which comes and goes repeatedly, rather than a once-occurring entity, in what would individuality finally consist? Would each example of the type really be an individual at all, or but one of an infinite number of copies? And more to the point for Christian doctrine, what would this mean for Jesus' atonement on the cross? Augustine argues that Jesus died once and only once to atone for human sins. A cyclical view, in which this event occurs again and again, would surely diminish the meaning of this sacrifice, and make a mockery of the idea of salvation. There could be no act of atonement which would take away human sin, if these sins are repeated again and again. Augustine concludes that upon a cyclical view of history, human beings would be consigned "to a ceaseless transmigration between delusive blessedness and real misery" (*City of God*, Book XII). True salvation requires the permanent expiation of sin, and true blessedness requires the assurance that the union of body and soul will be eternal.

The close and permanent connection of soul and body in Christianity made the body a focus of special attention. While Christians might be prepared to leave their disfigured or diseased bodies willingly enough or even to sacrifice their bodies for their faith, they do so with the thought that they will regain them in the afterlife. During life, a Christian cannot look at the body with the bemusement of a Greek or Roman philosopher, who supposes he will be done with it soon enough. The limitations which body imposes on soul for such thinkers are temporary, and thus one's actions need not be monitored continually. For a Christian the body is and will always remain present. The promptings of soul to satisfy itself through the senses of the body must be guarded against vigilantly. From this necessity, wildly divergent courses of

action have been pursued: some have chosen chaste family life; others celibacy; yet others mortification of the flesh or even self-castration. In every instance, however, the longings of soul to satisfy itself through sensual, bodily pleasure are not to be ignored, much less indulged, but must be seriously addressed in one way or another. The somewhat more relaxed Greek view of body gives way to the idea that the human body itself is a "temple," as Paul said, which can be defiled by the choices of human soul.

In this way, too, the consequences of wrong choices – the consequences of a human will turned away from God – are staggering. In opposing, and ultimately suppressing, every challenge to the eternal unity of each uniquely ensouled body, Christianity provided a solid and thoroughgoing foundation for the Western idea of the individual. To be sure, this reached its fullest social expression in the later Protestant versions of Christianity, which depreciated the importance of the corporate/communal/historical/institutional mediation of the church. But present in Christianity from the earliest years in which it fused together Greek and Hebrew views was a deeply implicit individualism. Individuals are not the standard by which God is judged; God judges individuals. But it is *individuals* which God judges, and in this regard Christianity set the stakes for every individual human being as high as they possibly could be. Human beings can choose to accept God's grace or they can turn their wills away from God. But each human being does so with his entire psychosomatic being. Each human being does so as a unique individual who will persist, for better or worse, forever.

FOUR

MIND:

ON EARLY MODERN BEING

How exquisitely the individual Mind to the external world is fitted, and how exquisitely too—Theme this but little heard of among men—the external world is fitted to the Mind...

William Wordsworth,
The Excursion

MIND:

ON EARLY MODERN BEING

The Greek dramatist Sophocles wrote, "What is unsought will go unfound." One must look in order to find. But more, one must somehow know in advance for what one is looking; how else how could one know one had found it? Thus far Sophocles and the Christian tradition travel together. But in Sophocles' formulation, there is no guarantee that one will find that which one is seeking. One could look and fail to find. Looking is a necessary, but not a sufficient condition of finding. Looking may well require thought and discipline, and perhaps even arcane kinds of knowledge, if what is sought is to be found.

As we have seen, the Christian view is different. "Knock and it will be opened" is a promise. "Seek and you will find" is a promise. Christianity offers the assurance that for those who seek, the truth will not be hidden. This is because the truth necessary to salvation lies open and readily at hand. There is no need for complex acts of intellection to find the truth, only an openness or a willingness to turn toward it. Truth does not lie veiled behind the world of appearances such that one must pass beyond appearances to a mental world available only to the few. It is there for the lowly, the simple, and the child-like. It is there because the world of appearances has been supplemented by the gift of revelation, which makes the truth clear to all who wish to see it. Truth is found in the choice of the will to assent to it, not in the depth of thinking. While Aquinas says that belief is an act of the intellect, he hastens to add that that act is

merely an assent to the "command of the will." The unfettered
mind – free from the good will which assents to God – might
indeed take one further from, not closer to, the truth.

We enter a profoundly different world in the early modern
period. Here we enter a world in which mind is set forward as
the essential characteristic of what it means to be human, as
that which places value on human beings and defines their
ends. To be sure, human beings still live in the everyday world
and still experience the multiple inputs of sense impressions
and of everyday wisdom. To be sure, the doctrines of revealed
religion still lie readily at hand. But the arbiter of truth, or of
what is most real, is not our senses; what is real lies behind
what our senses tell us, and access to that reality depends upon
our minds. Nor can truth be established by the simple assent of
our wills; whether our choices take us closer to or further from
reality can be judged only by our minds. Sensory input tells us
all that it ever has. Revelation unfolds to us all that it ever has.
But both the reality of the world, and the truth of the teachings
of revelation are to be judged by mind, not vice versa. The
value of human mind cannot be confirmed by its conformity to
our everyday impressions or to the teachings of revelation; to
the contrary, the value of our everyday impressions and of the
teachings of revelation must be confirmed by human mind.

The Primacy of Mind

The consequences of this view – which is a thoroughly
radical departure from Christianity – are revolutionary. They
include a new, and non-Christian, view of what can and does
count as real and of what is only apparent. They include a
fundamental alteration in the relation of human beings to their
own bodies. No longer do we have an unmediated relationship
to our own bodies, which are now understood to be a mindless
part of the external world. No longer can the direct experience

of our bodies (including suffering) offer an avenue to access what is most real about them. They include a new preoccupation with what can constitute knowledge and of how knowledge is possible at all, a preoccupation which philosophers later came to call epistemology. They include the vast expansion of the human ability to manipulate the external world (and our own bodies) to our own advantage – but at the price of reconstituting our place in the world in a new and rather forbidding way. The more able we are to manipulate the external world, including our own bodies, the more detached from this world we seem to become and the less the world seems like a home to us.

We will explore each of these consequences. For now, we observe in advance what is the conclusion of this analysis, namely, that early modern thought which arises in the sixteenth and seventeenth centuries (with earlier anticipations, to be sure) rests upon a thoroughgoing and fundamental *idealism*. This might seem surprising, given the ability which modern science offers human beings to manipulate the external world. It might seem surprising, too, because modern science does not – as do Christian teachings –warn against excessive preoccupation with the world around us. And it might seem surprising, too, in light of early modern thinkers who understood themselves – actually, often misunderstood themselves – to be "materialists." We shall see that quite often an announced philosophical materialism is the merest prejudice superimposed on what is at its core the thoroughgoing idealism upon which early modern thought rests.

We might gain an initial hint about modern idealism by observing the elevation of Plato in the early modern period. Why does it happen in the early modern period that Plato is everywhere elevated and Aristotle correspondingly depreciated? After all, conventional wisdom tells us that Plato is the author of

speculative flights of fancy and Aristotle the patient and systematic observer of nature. After all, Plato is the craftsman of open-ended moral dialogues from which many and competing lessons can be drawn, and Aristotle is the prosaic cataloguer of beings that are visible to the human eye and tangible to human touch. Does not the empirical Aristotle bring the speculative Plato down from the clouds and back to earth? Why then would Plato be so congenial to the new science of early modernity?

The relationship between Aristotle and Christian thinkers in the later middle ages is a broad subject, and its exposition need not be a part of our current enterprise. It will suffice here to say that the thinkers of the early modern period understood Aristotle to be a part of the intellectual system they aimed to overthrow. The question is not why they bundled Aristotle and medieval Christianity together, which is obvious enough; it is why they sought to overturn this system at all, and what role Plato plays in this endeavor. To say that Plato's manuscripts happened to be re-discovered and translated at this time would be to say far too little. What do Renaissance thinkers find in Plato that is so attractive?

Should we suppose that early modern thinkers lacked the courage simply to jettison all prior philosophical thought and strike out on their own? Or that these revolutionary thinkers lacked the courage of their convictions and needed to find support and justification for their enterprise by leaning on some ancient source, and that Plato was the convenient antidote to Aristotle? These men who overturned fifteen centuries of Christian doctrine in favor of deism – they lacked the intellectual courage and daring of their convictions?

The fact is that the core of the early modern intellectual enterprise was largely congruent with Platonic teachings, and early modern thinkers found in Plato a genuine philosophical ally. Novera, the teacher of Copernicus, found much to be

admired in Plato and passed along his enthusiasm to his students. So, too, did perhaps the most significant and consequential of all early modern scientists, Johannes Kepler. Kepler, who was the author of the new scientific understanding of the motion of the planets, was a dedicated sun worshipper and admirer of Plato. And so, too, were the many members of the Florentine Academy who found in Plato support for their new enterprise.

But perhaps the best testimony to Plato's importance is not the new philosophers and scientists at all, with their fondness for Plato's geometrical world. Even more telling is the deepest and most thoughtful *theological* response to the new science of early modernity: Cambridge Platonism. Here is a movement which was shaken out of its dogmatic slumber by the militant materialism of Thomas Hobbes. The Cambridge Platonists did not reject the new science, but accepted it. In seeking to reconcile the new science with Christian theology, they concluded that Hobbes had drawn exactly the wrong consequences from the new science. They found the implicit idealism of the new science, its Platonism, fully congenial with a spiritualized, idealized version of Christianity. In doing so, to be sure, they strongly accented a de-physicalized version of Christianity – but they understood better than Hobbes the character of the modern scientific enterprise. The world might be construed by its new expositors as a set of mathematical rules; it might be thought of as an emanation of God; or it might be understood as bodies behaving according to predictable, knowable patterns of motion. But no matter how understood, there is but one way to access such a world – and the patterns or rules which comprise it – and that is through the ideas of the human mind.

There is no clearer or more consequential exponent of the new thinking about man and the external world than Rene Descartes. An accomplished mathematician, Descartes turned

to consider what it is about mathematics that provides certain knowledge. In what does this certainty reside? Where can be found a firm footing on which to rest genuine knowledge, knowledge of what is unfailingly and everywhere and always true? His answer, of course, is not through the senses or the experiences of everyday activity. It is not from the experience of suffering or joy, no matter how forcefully these experiences present themselves. Nor is it through what has been said or written by others, no matter how venerable the source, how often repeated, or how long reaffirmed down through the centuries.

As is well known, Descartes finds the basis for certainty only within his own mind when it is thinking. An ancient school asserted that "man [kind] is the measure of all things;" for Descartes, his *own* mind is the measure of all things. Even when Descartes denies he is a thinking being, yet he is still thinking. And thus whatever else thinking may be, it is the guarantor of his existence and the ground upon which certain knowledge is to be found. But thinking guarantees more for Descartes than his existence. It guarantees as well that thinking is the essential human activity, that thinking is the essential characteristic of what it means to be a human being. In his *Meditations*, Descartes asserts flatly that "thought...alone is inseparable from my nature." Further on in the same treatise he reiterates this identity in saying "the real I, that is, my mind."

In equating mind with what is real about being human, Descartes distinguishes his view of mind from the Greek concept of soul. In the Greek view, thinking is held up as the highest and most fully and distinctively human activity of soul. But though thinking may be soul's most quintessentially human activity, human soul is certainly responsible for far more than thinking. As we have seen, human soul for the Greeks was the en-livener of human beings in all the ways

human beings are alive – in motion, in growth and decay, in sensation, in perception and in thinking. Descartes, however, collapses human soul entirely into mind; for Descartes human mind *is* human soul, no more and no less. He says pointedly in the *Meditations*: "the mind (or soul of man, between which I find no distinction)." In his *Discourse*, Descartes hives off all functions of soul other than thinking, and relegates these functions to a bodily world which is forever separate from thinking. He says: "...therefore I concluded that I was a substance whose whole essence or nature was only to think, and which, to exist, has no need of space nor of any material thing." This thinking "substance," which can exist outside of space and the material world altogether, is a far cry from the en-souled "rational animal" of the Greeks. The rational animal has become a thinking machine.

Descartes thus separates thinking from all other (merely) bodily activities in a radical way. Thinking is no longer to be conceived as one of, albeit the highest and most distinctive, activity of an en-souled human. It is the only true human activity, and human soul expresses itself in no other way. Now thinking, at least as we are familiar with it, seems always to take place in human beings who are bodies as well. What is the relationship of thinking, if any, to these bodies with (in) which it seems co-located? Here Descartes is neither as clear nor as consistent as he might wish. In its purest form, Descartes' doctrine suggests a complete and radical separation of thinking and body. For example, Descartes says in the *Meditations* "...it is certain that this 'I' [that is to say, my soul, by virtue of which I am what I am] is entirely [and truly] distinct from my body and that it can [be or] exist without it." To this end he seeks even to banish images, with their sense-laden quality, from what he understands as thinking. "Imagination," he says further, "is in no way necessary to my essence, that is to say, to

the essence of my mind." The essence of mind, which is the essence of the human being, is to be found in ideas and the relation of ideas in the mind – and not in sensing, perceiving, or even imagining. From this he concludes that it thus "follows that this ego, this soul, by which I am what I am, is entirely distinct from the body...."

But Descartes had a predictably difficult time maintaining the purity of a sense-less, body-less human being. After all, he said that he was a "substance," albeit one without need of space or of materiality. What is this substance? At one point in the *Meditations* Descartes identifies this substance with his body, saying that "my essence consists solely in being a body which thinks (or a substance whose whole essence or nature is only to think)." At another point Descartes says quaintly, almost apologetically, "I have a body with which I am very closely united." At other points Descartes suggests that human mind and body are so intimately connected that "a single whole is produced." And on occasion Descartes even slips back into the familiar idea of the human being as a kind of psychosomatic unity. He says "my body, or rather my whole self, in so far as I am composed of body and mind."

Having tried so radically to sunder body and mind, however, Descartes had little success bringing them back together. How mind and body, so described by Descartes, could influence one another was a problem he bequeathed to his contemporaries and successors, a problem which constituted the heart of philosophical inquiry for the next century.

From the fact that we can know with certainty only that we are mind, it does not follow that we are only mind. Perhaps Descartes would grant that readily enough. But Descartes is clear that mind is equivalent to soul and that there is no non-mental soul. How then are we to account for movement, for growth and decay, and for human sensations and perception

which soul had long explained in both Greek and Christian thinking? If soul is equivalent to mind – and if it is unclear, if not altogether mysterious how mind can move body – what accounts for the motion and activities of living bodies? In a world where rest was self-explanatory, but motion begged explanation, the continual intervention of soul and/or spirit was required. Without the intervention of soul or spirit acting through soul, the world would soon enough achieve a permanent state of lifeless rest. But Descartes' world was not like that. In his Galilean world, motion is of one and only one kind, and it as normal as rest. Motion begs no special kind(s) of explanation; as was later said, bodies in motion remain in motion until and unless a force is applied to stop them. Neither rest nor motion requires more or less explanation than the other. Mind (soul) does not cause or en-liven the movement of any part of the universe. Though mind (soul) may be the essence of human being, mind is not at all necessary for the operation of the world, which goes on without mind at all. Though mind can understand how this movement takes place, its patterns and its rules, mind (soul) is not responsible for it. Indeed, the world goes on in a mindless, or as we more often say, in a mechanistic way.

For Descartes – and for his many followers – human movement is perfectly able in principle (if not always so well in fact) to be explained and understood in the same way as are the movements of all other bodies in the universe. The movement of all parts of the universe, living beings and even human beings included, is uniform and alike. Different explanations are not required for different types of motion – plant souls, animal souls, human souls, and so forth –because all motion is fundamentally alike in its mechanical character.

We shall discuss the cause of this mechanical motion, and the place of God in this universe shortly. But for now we might

note that for both Descartes and his successors what is uniquely human and which cannot be understood by reference to the patterns of mechanical motion is thinking, or mind. This thinking-only human soul, which Descartes identifies as mind, is taken over by virtually every thinker of early modernity. The eminent scientist Robert Boyle, who thought as carefully about the philosophical basis of early modern science as any of his contemporaries, follows Descartes in flatly identifying human soul as mind. For Berkeley, a theologian and a man of devout Christian practice, soul and mind are synonymous. Berkeley says in his *Principles of Human Knowledge* that "this perceiving active being is what I call *mind, spirit, soul, or my self.*"* And so, too, Leibniz, who says in his "Principles of Nature and Grace" about human beings: "their souls are called *minds*. These souls are capable of acts of reflection, and of considering what we call myself, substance, soul, or minds."

Early modern science studied the patterns of motion of bodies in the external world. It was perhaps easy enough for popular consciousness to see in this a materialism, especially given the provocations of philosophers like Hobbes. But it was the reality of mind which comprised the essence of being human, as well as provided the key to unlocking the secrets of the motions of the physical world. These secrets were themselves patterns or relations or ideas, and in these ideas lay what was most significant both about the world and about human being. In drawing the anti-Hobbesian conclusion about early modernity's new project, the Cambridge Platonist, George Cudworth spoke a clarifying truth: "as if there were not as much reality in fancy and consciousness as there is in local motion." Here in early modernity is an idealism that might have made Plato blush.

---

* In his *Dialogues*, Berkeley says: "The being of my self, that is, my own soul, mind or thinking principle..."

The External World

For Descartes and his many and various followers, it was taken as certain that what mind can know best is itself and its own activities. What is most certain are the simple and clear intuitions that lie directly before the mind, unmediated by sense perception. There is no certainty to be found in the senses; that one thinks rather than that one suffers is the proof of one's existence. What is next most certain after direct intuition are complex intuitions that are patiently built up step by step from simple, direct intuitions. These complex intuitions, best exemplified by geometrical proofs, are not themselves immediately and intuitively obvious, but are derived by a process which at each stage is simple and obvious. This kind of certainty depends wholly upon the intuitive relationship of ideas with one another.

But what of our knowledge of the external world which presses in upon us through each of our senses, the world in which we live when we are not thinking about the relation of ideas to one another? How does our knowledge "jump across" from our mental manipulation of ideas to what seems, or at least seems to ordinary common sense, to lie outside the mind? How is knowledge of the external, sensible world possible, and in what could such knowledge possibly consist? Early modern science looked out upon the external world and, aided by mathematical tools, found there a series of regular patterns in its motion. Knowledge of these patterns seemed to improve vastly humanity's ability to operate in the world. Such knowledge could bring benefits to humanity in many walks of life. But these instrumental advantages, significant as they may be, do not themselves answer the question: what is the relation between the patterns of ideas in our minds and the external world? What, for example, is the relation of the ideas in our

mind which we call a gravitational theory and the reality of the external world?

Though one might find here an almost irresistible movement toward pragmatism in one form or another, these are not easy questions, and valiant philosophical efforts were made to answer them. Virtually all such answers of early modern philosophers, however, moved strongly in the direction of depreciating sensory impressions. Sense perception, after all, rightly and truly reports to humans that the sun "rises" in the east each day and then "sets" in the west. We had these perceptions before Copernicus and we have them still today. Is not the rising and setting of the sun "real" in this regard? Descartes and his followers would not deny the truth of our sensations about where in the sky the sun arises and sets each day – but for them there is no "reality" captured by these impressions. While no mathematical demonstration of a solar-centered world cancels out our ongoing sense impressions, these impressions cannot lead us to what is most real about the external world. Input from the senses may be straightforward and not mistaken, but any mental conclusions from these inputs are not. The mind goes astray when it reasons directly from sense impressions. Information drawn from the senses is indistinct, chaotic, and even misleading. Information from the senses can be a snare of delusion if it is taken in an unmediated way. Such information can lead us further away from what is most real about the external world.

What then is the connection between the certainty derived from our mental intuitions and the external world? Does not the very possibility of knowledge of the external world require that somehow our ideas and the external world (miraculously) mirror one another? Some thinkers backed into this conclusion gingerly, while others embraced it energetically. But it is the predicate of early modern thought that what is most real about

the external world is the very regularity which its motions display. This regularity – which of course is accessed by the mind's ability to relate ideas to one another – is constitutive of a world more real than the one that flows in through the senses. Kepler embraces this view with enthusiasm. He argues that the mathematical harmony which our minds are able to uncover in the external world is not only congruent with the ideas of our minds, but that this harmony lies "behind" and causes the external world to be just as it is and not otherwise. One sees the very definition of what is real transforming itself. Reality is no longer what is accorded the most self-sufficiency or the most efficacy, but reality is that which conforms to the relationship of our (mathematical) ideas. Mathematics is not just a helpful tool, but becomes itself the arbiter of what is most real. The method is no longer a useful assistant on the path to knowledge; the method is the master which defines both what counts as knowledge and what counts as reality. What is quantitative, or what is able to be understood quantitatively, is most real. As Kepler says, "Nothing can be known completely except quantities or by quantities...."

This view led to a predictable, but still striking, consequence. Certain characteristics that had long been imputed to the reality of the external world were now denied to be any part of that reality at all. These were the so-called "secondary qualities" of bodies. The qualities of taste and color and smell were concluded to be no part of what is most real about the external world, but to reside (merely) in the act of perceiving them. There is no redness in an apple apart from its being so perceived. Human beings – and perhaps other animals too – bring to the external world the capacity to sense which gives rise to secondary qualities which are constructed in our minds. As the unmediated products of sense perception, those qualities are indistinct and "subjective" and they are the source not of

knowledge, but of perpetual wrangling and disputation.

When the so-called secondary qualities were stripped from what is most real about the external world, all that remained was extension and motion – both of which were measurable. The mathematical measurement of the motion of extended bodies reveals, indeed comes to count as, what is most real about the external world. Here we find a most interesting vocabulary used to describe these measurable patterns. From Galileo onward, the regular patterns of the external world accessed by mind are typically called "laws" or "laws of nature." What could it mean to call the regular patterns of the external world "laws," and who or what is the lawgiver? After all, the term "law" is drawn from the human world of politics and governance. A "law" in a political order is what is set forth to bind all citizens, or at least all subjects. A law has a kind of general applicability in this sense. But of course there is an obvious problem: laws are often broken, or even ignored, by members of a political order. This is surely not the sense that is intended by a "law of nature," which suggests unswerving obedience with no deviation whatsoever. Bodies in motion are not at liberty to break, or to ignore, the laws of nature. The laws of nature are uniform and binding upon their subjects – same conditions, same result every time. What is meant by calling the recurrent patterns of nature "laws" rather than, say, "axioms" of nature, which might arguably have been a clearer description of what was intended?

The answer to this lies in the idea of "nature." Implicit in the unfailing rigidity of a law of nature is a new conception of nature altogether. Nature is no longer understood as that which grows and decays, which can be understood only in the approximate everyday way in which it expresses itself. Nature is neither the approximate patterns recognized in the Torah or the *phusis* of the Greeks or the physical world of Christianity.

"Nature" assumes a brand new meaning. As is sometimes the case, we can best appreciate this shift in meaning by considering what the new concept of nature is *not*. The true antonym of the early modern concept of "natural" is no longer "unnatural;" it is "artificial." Nature is what there is which is neither mind nor that which has been acted upon by mind. Nature is still that which is "given" to humans, as it had always been – but what is "given" has lost its entire sense of being given by a creative mind, by intentionality. Nature has lost its sense of meaningfulness. Nature is no longer a set of various processes, like growth and decay, which are humanly meaningful. Nature is the operation of the external world without the intermediation of mind, which is the wholly non-natural outsider. What is "given" to humans is what has extension and motion in space and time outside of any human action upon it.

As that which lies outside of and untouched by human mind, nature is thus completely – inhuman. Nature does not partake of the quality which defines what it means to be human, that is, mind. Nature is not of human art or contrivance; it lies before us as a neutral backdrop or surrounding within which human minds happen to find themselves. It is certainly not a "home" for human beings; it is a passive, non-caring mechanistic environment within which human mind must find its way as an outsider. The "laws" of this nature partake not at all of the interiority characteristic of human minds. They display a binding rigidity uncharacteristic of human law, a rigidity which is captured in the phrase "iron law."

Who or what is the lawgiver of such a natural world? Many answers ranging from careful agnosticism to a refined conventional theology were possible. But the one characteristic of the early modern God, or lawgiver, is that (if he exists at all) he has become less humanly accessible, less personal, and far

more transcendent. This God set the world of nature into motion and it now runs "on its own," as it were, according to the patterns which God established. Indeed, there was extended debate over the question whether God had constrained even himself in creating the natural world, that is, whether even God could alter his creation except by using the very laws according to which it operates. This God, best expressed in deism, is no personal God, but a distant transcendent being whose utility lies in a long distant creation and not in any contemporary acts. Among philosophers, Leibniz is an exception. He, too, finds unswerving regularity in nature, but argues that this regularity of nature is merely a "habit" of God, and that God can break the regularity of nature through a miracle whenever he wishes to do so. This view saves the omnipotence of God, but one would wrongly suppose Leibniz's God to be frequently in the business of breaking his own rules, even if he could. For Leibniz and for early moderns generally, where humans can meet and appreciate God is through the activities of their minds in grasping the regular patterns of the world of nature.

No matter how understood, reality is accessed by the ideas of our minds. What is most real about the external world are the invariant patterns of its motion. These, and these alone, can be known with certainty. Here we might offer a brief comment on empiricism in early modern thought. For if mind is the way to gain access to what is most real (and perhaps even to nature's God), mind is also capable of flights of fancy that take us away from what is real. After all, it was the oft-repeated criticism of scholastic thought that mind meditating on its own ideas created mental schemes lacking all utility and relation to "reality." Francis Bacon offered a fulsome catalogue of ways that mind could lead us away from reality, ways which he called "idols." In this regard, is it not the hallmark of early modern thought that it somehow tests its ideas against the

external world and does not merely spin out webs of words and ideas? Did not the work of Kepler and Galileo and Boyle and Newton stand or fall upon whether their theories were somehow "confirmed" by reference to the patterns of the external world? And in this regard it is the senses that seem to tell us that, yes, this ball falls at a certain speed, this gas expands to a certain volume, and this body attracts another with a certain force. How then can we speak of the implicitly idealist character of early modern thought, if the senses are everywhere the arbiters of what is and what is not occurring in the external world?

Sense perceptions flow into human beings in diverse and seemingly random ways. Depending upon one's immediate environment, sense perceptions of one or another kind stream into us. They are, in a manner of speaking, "given" to us by the external world. *These* sense perceptions, however, could neither confirm nor disconfirm any theory. What is required to confirm or disconfirm a theory is that mind should decide which sense perceptions are and are not relevant. Mind sets up a test case – an experiment – and argues that for a theory to be confirmed, certain logical conclusions are inherent within it. If one can observe these consequences then the theory is tentatively confirmed; if not, it is not. This process surely involves the senses, but the senses are under the careful direction of mind. As such, there is a tentative or provisional quality to all confirmed theories. No amount of sense data is ever sufficient to confirm a theory once and for all; if a logical consequence of a theory's truth is later discovered not to conform, the theory must be revised, for it is conformity to the unfailingly invariant patterns of nature that establishes its validity or lack of validity.

What are we to make of this conclusion? Hobbes asserts the most radical and least justifiable conclusion: the only reality is

"bodies in motion." He makes this conclusion despite the fact that, as he elsewhere shows, only the conformity to patterns of ideas in our minds could possibly tell us this is so. Hobbes does not anywhere show why ideas must be understood somehow to be bodies in motion, rather only asserting the truth of this view.

Berkeley came to a more justifiable, but opposite, conclusion from Hobbes. For Berkeley it is the givenness of our ideas that we *call* the external world. Berkeley argued that we have ideas of imagination and ideas derived from sense. Ideas derived from sense have a quality of givenness to them. Ideas of imagination have origins which are difficult to fathom, but for all of that could well be determined or fixed in some (unknown) way as well. What we call the external world are those ideas derived from sense which cohere in a logically and almost irresistible way.

Isaac Newton suggested a third way. Though he had every reason to be less modest than his contemporaries, he offered a more modest thought. He counseled that he would "frame no hypotheses" about what were the most real forces operating in the external world. He would content himself with what lay within the bounds of human comprehension, namely, knowledge of the way in which the patterns of the external world operate. We do not need to know exactly what gravity is, or why this might be what is most real about the external world, in order to know how gravity operates. Knowledge of how the patterns, or laws, operate, is as much knowledge of reality as is available to us through the work of our minds. We might choose to call these patterns reality, or not, but the salient point is this: this kind of knowing is the distinctive quality of human beings and the one through whose exercise we can come however close to reality as is possible for us.

Whether the Hobbesian, the Berkeleyan, or the Newtonian conclusion be drawn, if knowledge is to consist of more than

mental juggling, the relation of our ideas must conform to something outside of themselves.* This is surely the implication of Francis Bacon's dictum that nature, to be commanded, must be obeyed. We are not free to spin out our ideas as we please and to dictate how nature will operate. To the contrary, nature plays *its* part in dictating to us how we must proceed if we are to be its master. There was but one genuine solution, in many variations, to the question of how our ideas are related to the external world of extension and motion. It is ironic that a poet should go to the core presumption of the early modern world, but no one says better than William Wordsworth in his *Prelude*, VI, how it is that our minds and the external world happen to be "exquisitely fitted together" for one another. For Wordsworth this does not mean that mind aims slavishly to capture and reproduce what is external to it; mind, he says, is no "mere pensioner on outward forces." But neither does mind willfully compose an external world out of itself, as our modern contemporaries so readily claim to do. Rather, there is for Wordsworth and for early modern thought a special conformity and fittedness between mind and the external world. Whether so arranged by a benevolent god or not is perhaps hard to say. But for Wordsworth this fittedness makes knowledge of the external world possible and at once guarantees that it will be founded on the ideas of the mind and not the impressions of the senses. This happy coincidence is the source of all that is most fully human. We shall let Wordsworth (*Prelude*, XIII) speak to the core conviction of early modern thought when he says that the fittedness of mind and the external world for one another

---

* Only Thomas Reid avoids this issue. Like Newton, he argues that we cannot know why, but only how, things happen. But he solves the problem of how our ideas relate to the external world in a unique way – by denying we *have* any ideas of things in our minds.

occurs by means of "fixed laws whence spiritual dignity originates."

Mind and Body

Having divorced mind so sharply from the world of extended bodies, Descartes was at pains to describe how mind and the external world can interact with one another. This problem was especially acute with regard to one extended body in particular, namely, the human body which is somehow associated with mind. If of such radically different character, how can mind influence or act upon our own bodies? And how, if at all, does our body act upon our mind? Descartes sets this problem so squarely and so forcefully that much of 17th and 18th century philosophy is an extended attempt to answer this question.

The standard Christian answer to this dilemma would not suffice. The Christian view of influx, according to which spirits flow into human souls and so move human beings, was no longer an available solution. For Descartes, soul was no longer understood as a mediating or attuning instrument between spirits and body; soul was mind, pure and simple, possessed of only the power to think. And outside of mind there is no soul. All of what we call soul is contained in mind, and mind's sole and unique power is to think.

One response to Descartes' problem came to be known as "occasionalism," a doctrine designed to conform Cartesian philosophy and Christian theology. Upon this view, bodies and minds do not act directly upon one another. Rather, the activities of both body and mind are explained by reference to a third, outside force, which is God. Minds may think thoughts, but it is God that puts these thoughts into minds. Bodies may cause other bodies to move in a mechanical way, but it is God who is the source of this causation. This he does according to

the regular patterns of nature which we are able to discern. It may seem that human minds can cause human bodies to move, but there is no such causation. What occurs in the seeming conformity of mind and body – I think I will raise my arm, and my arm rises – is that God intervenes at every moment to create this parallel harmony between thinking and bodily motion. The bridge between human mind and human body is to be found in God. Occasionalism is no merely occasional intervention of God, but an ongoing, active, all-encompassing involvement of God in each and every occasion that occurs.

Occasionalism offered a view of the world which was consistent with early modern science, in that it did not deny that God acted according to knowable and regular patterns; it was consistent with Descartes' separation of mind and body; and it preserved, or arguably even enhanced, a role for God in the world. Yet it could never be more than a rather clever philosophical attempt to reconcile all these views, and a very cumbersome one at that. Against this view, Leibniz proposed his own view which had the virtue of far greater simplicity. Leibniz argued in his *Monadology*, #80 that there exists a pre-established (by God) harmony between body and mind, a harmony so clear that Leibniz believed that had Descartes known of the "conservation of direction" in matter he, too, would have subscribed to this harmony. When mind thinks that one's arm should rise, and one's arm rises, this does not require for Leibniz that God is actually intervening to create his harmony at that very moment. Rather, this and all other such harmony between thought and bodily motion that will ever occur were established once and for all by God in the universe which he created. One cannot help but note a certain parallelism between these two competing doctrines and the competing theological versions of the Christian eucharist. For occasionalists, the reality of God is actively present in each and

every circumstance of life. Liebniz, good Lutheran that he was, offers what we might call a kind of metaphysical consubstantiation, in which God need not be actively present in each and every circumstance, but is certainly somehow present alongside it.

Spinoza offered yet another solution. For Spinoza, too, neither body nor mind could leap across the abyss which Descartes had opened up. Spinoza said straightforwardly, even pointedly, that mind and body cannot influence one another. But this, he said, is because mind and body are not really two different kinds of entities at all, but simply (or not so simply) two different ways of looking at what is really one. Mind and body are two aspects, two ways of seeing, what is essentially one. Spinoza is quick to say that God thus moves the whole world every bit as fully as any occasionalist might assert. But what is less quickly, and more carefully implied is the reason for this: that God *is* the whole world, looked at as mind.

Each of these views, as well as other creative philosophical efforts, was defended by lengthy and subtle disputations, each pointing to specific advantages over the others. Perhaps Leibniz spoke most honestly in his *Discourse on Metaphysics*, however, in addressing the mind/body problem when he referred to "the great mystery of *the union of the soul* and *the body*."

The union of body and soul may be reconciled by one or another philosophical theory, or it may remain "mysterious." But however understood, the consequences of Descartes' radical separation of mind and body were substantial. For if human bodies are simply extensions in space, they will be subject to the very same laws of nature as are all other physical objects in the external world. This, and thus the possibility of human behavioral science, was not denied by any early modern philosopher. However each philosophical system aimed to

reconcile the worlds of mind and body, none rejected the idea that as bodies we humans are subject to the very same laws of nature as are all other physical objects. We are subject to the laws of gravity, the conservation of energy, and all the other laws or patterns of the external world. God may have created these patterns, but in his wisdom he did not choose to distinguish between human bodies and any other kinds of natural bodies. Here Descartes had already pointed the direction in arguing that animals are essentially machines, operating according to the mechanical laws of nature. There is no "animal soul" which accounts for a specific animal-like set of activities; animals are like any other part of extended nature. There is no "plant soul" which accounts for the specific kind of motion which plants display; plants are simply a part of extended nature. Descartes pointed the way to the quest to reduce all knowledge of motion to one kind of knowledge, which he took to be knowledge of mechanics.

So it is, too, with human bodies. It is not only the case that human beings are not "at home" in the world; human beings are not even "at home" in our own bodies. Human bodies, like any other kind of body, are a part of the physical world of extension, and true knowledge of human bodies must be sought in the same way as knowledge of any other natural body. Human beings do not enjoy reliable, trustworthy knowledge of their own bodies; there is no direct shortcut to knowledge of our own bodies. Our sensations are no more or less reliable sources of knowledge of our own bodies than of any other body. The truth about our bodies is not revealed through emotion or suffering but through the mediation of the ideas of the mind. This truth about human bodies we call "human nature." Broadly speaking, nature is what is given to us outside of and prior to being acted upon by mind. Human nature is what is "given" to us in the same way – it is of human beings

prior to, or independent of, being somehow shaped by mind. It is a life that looks very much like the life of an animal.*

Early modern philosophers developed a name for this kind of life, which they called the "state of nature." The state of nature is life as it would exist prior to the application of mind to shape or guide it. It is life without recourse to what Leibniz calls abstract knowledge. It is life which exists independently from, and not under the tutelage of mind. Since we have little or no direct experience with such life, early modern thinkers inferred what such life must be like either from thought experiments or from the limited knowledge they possessed about the lives of "savages." Life in the state of nature might look more or less happy, depending upon whether Hobbes, or Locke, or Rousseau is describing it. But it always expresses the character of human life prior to or independent of the application of mind.

To the extent that human bodies persist, they will always remain a part of nature. Mind can never eradicate the effects or qualities of human life that derive from our animal bodies. Mind has no more power to abolish (or educate or train out of us) these qualities than it does to abolish any other physical law or pattern of nature, such as gravity. Mind can never cause the characteristics of human nature to disappear. Mind can understand the operation of the laws of gravity and make use of

---

* Leibniz says it is abstract knowledge which ultimately separates humans from animals: "...the knowledge of necessary and eternal truths is what distinguishes us from mere animals and gives us *reason* and *science*, rising us to the knowledge of ourselves and of God. And that is what is called a *rational soul, or a mind*." (*Monadology*, #29). In an amusing remark, Leibniz goes on to quantify how often we act like humans and how often like animals, or beings without minds. He says that neither movement, nor memory, nor the ability to associate a present situation with a past one – capacities we share with animals – but only the ability to see necessary truths inherent in the relation of ideas makes us humans. Leibniz estimates we act like animals about three-fourths of the time.

this knowledge for its own purposes – but it cannot abolish the law of gravity. Likewise, mind can understand the characteristics of human nature and use this knowledge to create new and different kinds of institutions – but it can never transform human nature itself. Early modern political thought, for example, aimed to utilize the knowledge of human nature to construct a new kind of government. This government accepted human nature as it was; it aimed to make a virtue of necessity. That this approach should come to dominate the early modern world was not a result of an otherwise inexplicable desire to "aim lower" than the ancients, from Machiavelli onward. Machiavelli offered no more or less than was in fact available to and advocated by any ancient sophist. It was a result of the Cartesian separation of mind and body, which relegated human nature to the uneducable, unalterable world of nature.

That mind can operate on the bodily world only indirectly has several other significant consequences. First, it reframes the issue of human freedom. As we have seen, Christian doctrine grants to human beings some interior latitude to act, some degree of freedom of the will. To be sure, the reach of this freedom remains limited by the inherent tendency of post-fall humans to sin and even by God's gift of grace itself. Even as Christians wrestled with the question of how free the human will is, they always supposed it to be sufficiently free (and unmoored from the goodness of God's creation) to merit damnation as a result of sin. How can there be even this degree of freedom for an early modern thinker if the human mind has no way to influence its body, if it cannot cross over the chasm that Descartes opened? For the early modern thinker the body is buffeted about by the forces of the external world as fully as it is for an ancient Greek philosopher. Indeed, more so; now it is not moved about randomly or by forces that come and go mysteriously (and might be called gods or demons), but by

forces of persistent and inalterable rigidity. How could mind affect such a world which acts according to fixed and immutable patterns, whether established by a distant god or not? Mind cannot even flatter itself that its vehicle on earth, its body, is moved about by any special or uniquely human life-forces.

For that matter, how free is human mind to shape its own interior world of ideas? Does mind enjoy the effective power to bring into consciousness and to relate ideas at *it* pleases? And what is the "it" that pleases to do so? Does human mind have the latitude to think as it pleases, or do ideas come to mind as *they* please? If there is to be any freedom at all for an early modern thinker, it must be within one's mind. But how, and to what degree that freedom exists is difficult to fathom. Early modern thinkers move toward taking back even that partial and uncertain grant of freedom offered by Christian doctrine. They move toward a conclusion which, like so many of the tendencies of early modern thought, is thought through by Immanuel Kant. Minds may be free – and thus in some measure humans may be free – but only if they are operating according to the world of necessity which is given to them. Minds cannot and do not act with freedom in a random and spontaneous way; they act freely only when acting in accord with the abstract rules of necessity. Freedom is never exercised in a specific, discrete way in a specific, discrete circumstance. If we are to act freely, we must do so without regard to our immediate circumstance or situation. We must abstract from it all particularity and act according to what is abstractly and generally true. Our freedom is very narrowly determined. And our minds, which are the essence of human being, seem to have no age, no gender, no race, and no nationality. When acting freely, mind has no greater love for what is near than what is far, for one's own family than any other family, for one's own

tribe than any other tribe. If mind is to shape in any way the external world of extension in which it finds itself, it must do so by acting consistently with the given patterns or laws (which it discovers, to be sure) of the external world.

This leads to a second significant consequence: early modern thought undercuts the Christian notion of salvation, the Christian doctrine of eternal salvation or damnation of the entire psychosomatic being. This consequence, implicit already in Descartes, is explicitly drawn by John Locke. Locke denies that personal identity does or can have anything whatsoever to do with bodily continuity. He argues in his *Essay on Human Understanding* (Book II, XXVII) that personal identity is equivalent to the mind's continuing awareness of itself, which we call self-consciousness. Personal identity extends as far – but only as far – as consciousness extends:

> Self is that conscious thinking thing – whatever substance made up of, (whether spiritual or material, simple or compounded, it matters not) – which is sensible or conscious of pleasure and pain, capable of happiness and misery, and so is concerned for itself, as far as that consciousness extends.

Locke argues that while such a "person" may be resurrected, and while an awareness of pleasure and pain might require a body, resurrection need not require the same body in which that person existed on earth. Locke asserts that the changes which occur to our bodies in this world in no way affect what it means to be a person. It will matter no more or less in a future world. Locke draws his most far-reaching anti-Christian conclusion: eternal salvation or damnation may be meted out to selves, or persons who are the same as those that did the actions which are judged, but "in whatever bodies soever they appear, or what substances soever consciousness

adheres to...." Locke completes the break-up of the Christian psychosomatic being. Body is depreciated to a mere arbitrary vehicle, as a substance to which consciousness "adheres." A final judgment may or may not occur; but if it does, it will judge the "person" which is the mind's persisting awareness of itself, that is, consciousness. If eternal rewards or punishments are to consist of physical pleasure or pain, Locke grants readily enough that mind must again adhere to some body. But which body it matters not, for body is merely a substance to which consciousness adheres, in this life or in any other.

The Power of Mind

To this point, we have stressed the independence of the human mind from the world of extension in time and space. Mind may (or may not) be free to operate in the realm of ideas, but its ability to operate in the world of extension must take place according to fully fixed and determined rules or laws which mind discovers, but which it has no power to shape. The external world is given to us; it is not an environment which we are free to mold, much less one that we have created. It ran before we were present and it will continue unchanged after we are gone. Early modern philosophy may have depreciated our bodies as mere vessels at every turn – but they took their revenge, as it were, by operating according to laws which our minds cannot alter in any way. The world of extension in time and space is a cold and impassive place to which appeal cannot be made. It must be accepted on its own terms.

Moreover, our minds have no access to receive the truth about the world through a source outside of thinking. There is no special faculty for receiving the truth of revelation, as opposed to the truth, or the certainty, which emerges from thinking. Revelation consists of the written and oral reports of others, and reliance on such outside sources – no matter how

ancient, how self-assured, or how seemingly authoritative – has no higher standing than reliance on any other reports from the world of sensation. No longer is it the task of thinking to uncover ways in which revelation is true and convincing, and thus to provide support for it. To the contrary, revealed truths must now demonstrate that *they* are reasonable, or at least consistent with the truths derived from the human mind – or they will themselves be rejected. What God may reveal to humans is of course the truth; but whether something is a divine revelation or not, only the human mind can judge.

John Locke's *The Reasonableness of Christianity* takes just this stance; the claims of Christian revelation are judged by their conformity to human reason. A book entitled *The Christianness of Reason* would have implied a different standard, one by which the truths of human thinking are judged at the bar of revealed truth. As it stands, however, the claims of revelation must be judged by thinking human minds, and whatever cannot so justify itself has no validity. Revelation does not work side-by-side with human thinking, each supplementing the other; to the contrary, whatever is not reasonable has no standing. At its best, revelation is a kind of picture book to help those of limited ability to understand, but it is in no way a genuine assistant to reason or thinking.

Early modern Christian philosophers did not doubt the ability of God to do miracles, that is, to alter the regular pattern of motion of the extended world. But even they were not inclined to believe that the Christian God was a mercurial god who would frequently intervene in special cases. To the contrary, they were much impressed by the wisdom of God in creating the regularity of the world, and believed that his general wisdom would regularly trump his specific mercy. Herein lay the explanation for the results of evil and for the

claim that, on the whole, the imperfect world is the best of all possible worlds.

So strong was this tendency that knowledge of God himself was to be sought in the human mind itself. To be sure, one might appreciate something about the majesty of God by observing the regularities of the external world. But knowledge of God himself was not best sought in the external world, but in the human mind itself. Perhaps no one better represented the broadly shared wisdom of early modernity than Lord Herbert of Cherbury, the "father of deism." Here is Lord Herbert's counsel: "Retire into yourself and enter into your own faculties; you will find there God…" God is not to be found in his mighty acts – not in the exodus from Egypt, or the incarnation, or the final judgment. God is to be found as an idea in the human mind. As Lord Herbert counseled, early modern theology turned inward to learn about God. This is reflected in the "inner certitude" of the Cambridge Platonists, in the inner light of the Friends, and in deism's creator God who set the world running according to the fixed patterns or laws which it displays.

Human beings thus cannot break out of the immanent world which we inhabit. Transcendent truths that surpass human thinking might or might not exist; but if they do, they are not and never will be available to human beings except through the relations of ideas within human minds. Moreover, the mind itself can be misled, and can misrelate sensations to create false conclusions. It can reason wrongly from step to step and arrive at faulty inferences. Mind can deceive itself about what it accomplishes in its thinking. Because there are no intrinsically reliable direct reports from the external world and no intrinsically reliable assistance from revelation, mind is on its own, as it were, to reason as best as it can. This puts a premium on understanding what counts and what does not

count as genuine knowledge. Philosophy turns away from the external world and inward upon itself and becomes ever more closely identified with what is called epistemology, or theory of knowledge. The Cambridge Platonist George Cudworth first used the world "epistemonical," by which he meant that which is capable of becoming an object of knowledge. By the mid-nineteenth century the word "epistemology," the study of what does and does not count as knowledge, came into currency. We see what a distance we have traversed from the ancient Greek world. The Greek word from which "epistle" is derived meant to send a report on a given occasion. In the modern world all such reports are suspect, and the sense of the current word "epistemology" is completely the opposite of its original root. Philosophy as epistemology is philosophy which *suspects* the validity of all external reporting. Philosophy as epistemology is the philosophy of human beings whose essence is no longer at home in the external world.

But this is only one side of the story. For while mind may not be at home in the natural world of extension in space and time, mind has ways in which it can gain power over that world. The cunning of reason provides human mind with considerable power over the external world. Francis Bacon, who catalogued the numerous ways in which the human mind can be misled, nevertheless in *The New Organon*, calls mind a "kind of divine fire." Bacon's intellectual endeavor displays itself as a humble one; he argues that mind should not aim to rise too high. Mind should stoop, not soar. But embedded in the apparent humility of Bacon's project is an altogether different goal: "to extend more widely the limits of the power and greatness of man." This tower of Babel-like project was precisely what the books of Moses warned against.

How can mind extend and widen the power of man? Mind does this by a form of self-discipline, a harnessing of itself to a

set of rules and processes which will extend human knowledge. But who is the agent who establishes these rules and processes? It is mind itself. Who or what is the arbiter of what does and what does not conduce to extend human knowledge? It is mind itself. Within the apparent empiricism of Bacon's approach, mind is everywhere the explorer, the discoverer, and the arbiter. Leibniz might well have spoken for early modern thought generally, including the so-called empiricists, when he proclaimed in the *Discourse on Metaphysics* that "a single mind is worth the whole world."

In the book of Genesis, Yahweh gives value and worth to the world by shaping it from the formless void. In the seventeenth century John Locke offers the human version of this story. The world of nature, he says, lies all around. But it lies fallow, and it has no worth or value. It is only by virtue of the intervention of human mind that nature gains value. Locke says in his *Second Treatise on Government*, "For tis Labour indeed that *puts the difference* of value on everything." The natural state, the "state of nature," is pure potential, but with no actual value. Only when mind acts upon nature through the mindful intentionality of human labor, does nature fulfill its potential. When mind can fathom the regularities and patterns of nature, mind's power is magnified exponentially.

As mind applies itself to the actions of human beings – to human nature – humans learn to differentiate themselves from nature, including animals and other human beings. This is mildly appreciated by Hobbes; thoroughly admired by Locke; and understood as the principal cause of human misery by Rousseau. But however evaluated, all agree that the action of mind upon nature generally, and upon human nature specifically, is decisive. As mind learns more truly the patterns of natural bodies, including human bodies, this allows humans to magnify the differences between themselves and the external

world and between themselves and each other. Mind sets before human beings intricate ways in which we can envision and expand our desires and also shows ways that these desires might be satisfied. Human beings can in this way move beyond the limits of human nature – not by abolishing or ignoring the laws of nature, but by understanding them and using them in the service of their own ends.

In a complex process, mind teaches that human beings must sublimate their desires (which mind has helped to expand in the first place) in order to achieve the fullest range of their desires. This thought comes to it purest practical fruition in the American Constitution. This grand "experiment" was intended to test, and aimed to confirm, mind's proper understanding of human nature and mind's capacity to act upon it. Mind instructs that the natural inclinations of humans cannot be altered, but can be balanced against one another so a new and better outcome is possible. Such balancing is not easy, and it is certainly never finished, for there is no human evolution to a place where the natural traits of human beings will disappear. So long as humans are subject to the laws of nature, that is, so long as they have a nature – as beings extended in time and space – no anarchic utopia is possible. This is the sense of James Madison's statement that if, and only if, men were angels (that is, had no bodies), government would be unnecessary to achieve human ends. Humans can never escape the necessity of employing their minds to guide the ways in which they manipulate nature generally, and human nature specifically. But this power is no small thing. Though given to grand overstatement, Thomas Paine often best captured what moved and inspired his early modern contemporaries. In referring to the human power to shape our own governance, Paine offered the sweeping pronouncement that "we have it in our power to begin the world over again."

We have spoken of the state of nature and of the laws of nature. From Hobbes onward, it was often said that human beings also enjoyed certain "natural rights." In any customary sense of the word "right," however, a natural right is the one thing which no human being in the state of nature could possibly possess. Hobbes gives this away in the unusual manner in which he defines a natural right. A natural right, Hobbes says in *Leviathan*, "is the liberty each man hath, to use his own power, as he will himself, for the preservation of his own nature." He adds that *"naturally every man has right of everything."* This kind of right is in fact the right, or perhaps better said the obligation to be what one is. It is the same kind of "right" that water has to run downhill. As a natural creature, human beings are subject to natural laws; to call this subjection a "right" is merely to add an ideological affirmation, and a misleading one at that, to such a life. Later thinkers aimed to found the idea of natural rights on other bases, including as gifts from God – though with no more convincing grounds than Hobbes who at least if he spoke misleadingly, spoke directly. It was not until Kant founded the idea of natural right fully upon mind, that a clear (though perhaps no more convincing) basis for human rights was established. For Kant, the overarching "right" of mind is to be treated differently than nature, to be treated as having its own ends rather than acting under the compulsion of natural laws.

Mind is what allows human beings to turn the laws of nature to their own advantage. This is ironically true even for Hobbes who, having depreciated every non-tangible entity as unreal, concludes that it is the mind of man which – by virtue of its ability to know the laws of nature – allows human beings to alter their surroundings to maximum possible advantage. To add that mind consists of nothing but particles in motion does not add anything of consequence to this understanding. What is

of consequence for self-described materialists such as Hobbes as well as for early modern thinkers generally, was the thought that a mind properly attuned to the laws of nature can manipulate the natural world to its own advantage.

Though the manipulation of the natural world was the core project for mind in the early modern period, early modern thinkers did acknowledge at least one way in which mind related to nature in a different manner. Mind can relate to nature instrumentally, to be sure; but mind can also look upon nature with no specific goal or end in mind. Such a disinterested view of nature is called by early modern thinkers "aesthetics." This is a complement to the technological, instrumental approach to nature. There is considerable charm to this, but at the same time an aesthetic approach is simply the other side of a technological approach to nature. The two are part and parcel of one another; both are ways in which human mind relates to a natural world in which it is not at home. Would a culture which saw spirits everywhere moving the world, including themselves, adopt a disinterested, "aesthetic" standpoint toward the world? No more so than it would ever have occurred to an ancient Greek to look upon the cosmos with no "end" in mind, that is, disinterestedly, as if he were somehow miraculously no part of the cosmos and unmoved by *eros*.

Alongside the expressionless mechanical world of nature, there sparkles the jewel of the human mind. This mind can create within itself a world of ideas. This mind can uncover whatever can possibly be known about God or the gods. And, if properly oriented, this mind can exercise great power over the natural world. Mind has the ability to penetrate to the real processes according to which the natural world operates, and thus permits human beings to use these processes for their own ends.

We shall turn again to Wordsworth to say what is the open

secret of early modern thought which gives such power and glory to the human mind. And that is the underlying compatibility between the processes of the external world and the mind of man. The external world does not shape our minds or give them their power. Nor, as we shall soon see with our modern contemporaries, does the human mind create the external world. The mind's free creations are fantasies. But the mind's most valuable creations are decidedly not acts of fantasy, but are creations which display the implicit harmony which exists between mind and nature. Wordsworth points toward the contemporary view which presses idealism toward its fullest expression. But he remains rooted in the early modern world, where it is the discipline of the mind to seek out the harmony it shares with the external world. Here for Wordsworth, as for early modern thinkers generally, lies the highest human task. Here is where neither mind nor nature is depreciated, but both are elevated. Here is where, as Wordsworth says in his Preface to the Second Edition of "Lyrical Ballads," can be seen "man and nature as essentially adapted to each other, and the mind of man as naturally the mirror of the fairest and most interesting properties of nature."

FIVE

EGO:

ON BEING TODAY

The soul superstition which, in the form of the subject
and ego superstition, has not even yet ceased
to do mischief.

Friedrich Nietzsche,
Beyond Good and Evil

EGO:

ON BEING TODAY

Wordsworth's conclusion that the mind and the external world are exquisitely fitted together was a happy one. It expressed the full optimism that we, as human minds, could learn the true order of the universe. Though we may not be quite at home in this universe, our thinking can still provide us real knowledge and mastery over its processes.

Wordsworth's happy conclusion was not fated to last, for it contained within itself the seeds of its own destruction. Wordsworth's conclusion begged the question: why should it be that our minds and the external world are so happily fitted together? That God should have created this arrangement was of course one possible explanation. Though not provable, this explanation, in its many manifestations, had the virtue of not being disprovable in any ordinary way. Moreover, it softened the background of the mechanical processes of the universe in which we find ourselves.

But other answers were available as well, and Immanuel Kant had already advanced one such answer with extraordinary force and intellectual rigor. Kant drew the conclusion that it is the very way in which we know that shapes and determines what can be known. That we know is no happy coincidence that is bequeathed to us; that we know is a result of how we know, of what it means to know. Though it may seem obvious, it is profoundly obvious that our knowledge is and forever will be constrained by the rules according to which thinking operates. Were we to know in a different manner, what we can

and would know would be different. Kant's insight had the same effect as Descartes' a century earlier: it was the inescapable starting point for generations of thinkers.

Still, Kant himself never seemed to doubt that there was some reality, some X, which is "given" to us, that is, which lies outside of or external to our knowledge. But this is just Kant's point. Of this "reality," if this is even an appropriate word, nothing at all can be known. This reality exists for itself alone (*an sich*) and not for us. It is inaccessible to us. Kant explains why Newton's instinct, that he should frame no hypotheses about this reality, is sound. It is sound because this "reality" does not and cannot manifest a knowable structure. Indeed, though it lies beyond our understanding, it does not lie outside our minds at all, but is (simply) an idea of our minds. It is an idea about which nothing in particular can be thought, other than that it is. The force of this insight was irresistible, and modern thought has followed it out in countless ways. Though contemporary scientists often assert a materialist conclusion, this conclusion in no way informs the character of modern science, which operates in a fully Kantian spirit. It is not too much to say, as does Windelband in his *History of Philosophy*, that following Kant's *Critique of Pure Reason*, "Being is to be thought only in consciousness, only as a kind of consciousness."

How then is the human way of being to be understood? Human being is essentially thinking being, or mind, for Kant, just as for his early modern predecessors. But it is mind of a very certain or particular kind. For Kant, the essence of being human consists in the capacity to follow the rules of thinking. These rules he calls the "transcendental ego." The human being is essentially human because of our ability to follow or to conform to the given rules according to which knowledge is possible. The unifying, categorizing functions of thinking are what comprise the so-called transcendental ego, and we are

able to know by virtue of our capability to follow its rules.

Kant proceeds to draw the consequences for human action. Like his early modern predecessors, Kant understands that human beings are a mixture or an alloy of inclination (desire) and thinking, of body and mind. But he draws the sharpest possible distinction between inclination and thinking. Inclination, or desire, is always predicated upon the specific situation of a human being in space and time, with a body, a family, a history, and so forth. Action on the basis of inclination, even though it may make use of instrumental reason to fulfill its desire, is not genuinely human action. Rather (reminiscent of Leibniz), it is the activity of an animal, bound closely to its body, its place and its time. Genuine human action – what Kant calls moral action – must transcend all particulars and be founded upon thinking. Only that action which can be willed to be universal, regardless of all specific circumstances, is moral. This is sometimes called a non- or anti-consequentalist ethical theory, because it predicates morality on the purity of intention and not upon the consequences of action. But in a way, Kant's could be considered the most thoroughgoing consequentalist ethical theory imaginable. Do not choose because it might result in a good consequence in this instance; choose only that which one could wish would result in a good consequence in each and every imaginable case. For that matter, it is strange to imagine any non-revealed ethical theory in which consequentialism does not appear at some point, whether overtly or surreptitiously.

What is essentially human is to be found in setting aside one's specificity, one's uniqueness, and one's particularity in favor of action according to maxims that can be willed to be universally valid laws. Here the uniqueness of each and every human being is thoroughly depreciated in favor of thinking, which takes us beyond our unique and special circumstances.

The individual who achieves most fully his or her humanity is an interior individual whose thoughts and actions are unsullied by any happenstance, accidental, or less than universalizable quality.

This is a complete inversion of the original tribal sense of ethics. Ethics is no longer to be found in what is appropriate, that is, in favoring one's own. Ethics is now thoroughly abstracted. Indeed, taking special care of one's own is precisely the kind of action which is not permitted in Kant's ethics. Moral choices are choices made by conforming one's will according to thinking, according to what is valid everywhere and always and not only useful in the immediate circumstance.

For Kant, all beings in the universe achieve their essence – become what they most truly are – by following laws. But there is a fundamental difference between beings which can act according to thought and those which cannot. A stone does not roll down hill because it has chosen to do so. Nor does an animal choose its course of action either; an animal may think instrumentally about how to achieve its goal, but its goal is not chosen, but is given to the animal. Only beings capable of abstract thinking are capable of choosing their goals or ends. As beings capable of thinking, humans have the capacity to act freely and not blindly under the kind of compulsion which moves non-thinking beings. Here Kant elevates the concept that will become so central in contemporary thought: freedom. In so far as we are thinking beings, we humans are free.

But we might note that for Kant this grant of freedom is not as generous as it may at first appear. Humans are not free when acting out of inclination or desire. Humans act freely only when acting according to what could be willed to be a universalizable maxim. One might say of Kant's view that humans can choose to be free, but if they do not, they are not free. And if humans choose to be free it is only by following

maxims that can be willed to be universalizable laws. For Kant, all beings – including human beings – invariably act according to laws; they may do so under blind, unknowing compulsion or, as thinking beings, by choosing to follow laws. But it is the fate of all beings, including human beings, to act according to law.

As thinking beings, humans thus have the choice to be shaped by external forces or to be free, that is, to shape themselves and their actions according to laws. The centrality of freedom and of human choice will be taken up with a vengeance by Kant's successors. But for Kant, freedom is no capacity to act willy-nilly. It can be achieved in one and only one way and that is through thinking which aligns a human being with what could be willed to be a universal law. Freedom is founded upon thinking; unless one follows the rules of thinking, one remains stuck at the level of external compulsion. And where there is compulsion, there is no freedom and thus no realization of humanity's essence. For Kant, unlike his successors, our practical reason seems at times to reign supreme, but ultimately remains fully in tow to our pure reason. It is only in thinking, and in acting according to the universalizable laws that thinking dictates, that we find and actualize our freedom.

From Pure Reason to Practical Reason

There is implicit in Kant's thought a very deep tension. The external world (the noumenal world) seems to lie outside of and independent of our human world. It lies beyond our ability to know, cloaked in obscurity. It is somehow "given" to us, but in a way that is not at all useful to us. Yet it turns out that the external (noumenal) world which lies at the base of our possible knowledge is also an idea of our thinking itself. As an idea of thinking, it may not be our creation, but it is certainly

our idea. Kant maintains this tension throughout his work. But Kant's successors invariably drew conclusions which emphasized the perspective that the external (noumenal) world is simply an idea of our thinking. As an idea, it loses the "independence" of its externality. As a product of the rules of thinking, the external world becomes a creation of mind itself. The transcendental ego is revealed as the sole and unique creator not only of the possibility of human knowledge, but of the existence or being of the external world itself. The story of the movement from the primacy of pure reason to the primacy of practical, creative reason is the story of the contemporary world's self-understanding.

The first to draw these consequences from Kant's thinking were Schelling and Fichte. Schelling's first book, written in 1795, was entitled *The Ego*. Here he places the ego, the capacity to choose (which was so closely constrained for Kant) at the center of the world. It is the transcendental ego, now renamed the absolute ego, which is responsible for, or provides the ground of, all Being. Schelling elaborates upon this ego:

> *Its essence is freedom*, that is the ego cannot be considered except insofar as it posits itself through its absolute power as pure ego and not as any *Thing*. This freedom may be positively determined for we wish to ascribe Freedom not to anything-in-itself but to an Ego which is pure and autonomous, present to itself and excluding all non-ego.

The purely autonomous ego is unique; it stands apart from and over and above all else there is. It is not merely an idea necessary to our thinking; it is the creator and guarantor of Being. Its capacity is to be able to know itself (here is a formulation that takes us well beyond Kant) for what it is; when it does this, it realizes its essence. What then of the so-

called external world, the world of nature? Schelling seems to preserve something of the happy parallelism of Wordsworth's formulation; for Schelling, nature reflects consciousness. But it does so in a new and very different way. In a remarkable and radical formulation, Schelling argues that nature is nothing more or less than ego in the process of becoming (aware of) itself. Nature, or the external world, is here robbed of the last vestige of its independence of mind. From the Kantian world – where we can be free only when we choose to be free, and only then by following laws given to ourselves – we have leapt to a new world. In this world, ego *is* free, and all conceptions that it is not are only demonstrations that ego has not yet understood itself correctly and realized its own essence. All limitations on ego are the result of misunderstanding. The world comprised of things for themselves (*an sich*) and things for us (*fuer sich*) has collapsed into a world thoroughly for us, because it is a creation of ego itself. Humanity is no longer embedded within a world in which we cannot know things as they really are. Behind the appearance of the external world lies the creative/destructive power of ego itself. When ego knows itself, it abolishes the possibility of any world but the one(s) it creates. And so, too, it is possible to bring an end to our alienated feeling of not being at home in the world. It is our ignorance of ego's full creative freedom that has caused our alienation; when this is overcome, so too will be our alienation.

Fichte approaches these questions somewhat differently, but arrives at the same destination. Like Schelling, Fichte eliminated any and all independent basis for the reality of the external world. The external world arises out of the act of being posited by ego. The external world is a kind of "resistance" which is posited by ego, without which ego would be unable to know itself. Ego is like a muscle, which must confront resistance in order to develop. Ironically, however, when ego

posits the external world, it does so in a way in which the external world seems to operate according to deterministic causes and effects, that is, completely binding laws of necessity. This is the standpoint of the understanding. From the standpoint of the understanding, the external world does indeed act according to rigid and unbendable laws. Thus has ego created a prison of necessity for itself and for all else there is (that is, all else it posits). This is the world of science, of determinism, and of law-like behavior.

Yet, after all, it is ego that creates this world. Ego creates the world; the world does not create ego. As such, from the standpoint of practical reason the ego is the creative force behind the external world. This leaves no doubt about the priority of pure (theoretical) reason or practical reason; practical reason is prior and any other conclusion is an alienated misunderstanding of the essential freedom of ego. For Fichte, practical reason teaches that external reality is a free creation of ego. Juergen Habermas says that for Fichte there is a unity of pure and practical reason. There is truth to this, but it would be more accurate to say that pure reason is a kind of practical reason; pure reason is practical reason operating as it does when it creates the world of nature, of laws, and of sheer determinism. When ego understands itself fully, it understands that the world of ordered, law-like appearances is its own creation. The natural or positive sciences aim to understand the processes of this ordered, law-like world. But the higher science of knowledge (*Wissenschaftslehre*) reveals that all Being, in the words of Windelband, is ultimately to be found in the "relation of consciousness to itself."

Schelling and Fichte were the first who aimed to draw out and elaborate upon Kant's philosophy; there were many others. Friedrich Jacobi, for example, accepted Kant's premise that conceptual knowledge cannot take us to reality. In lieu of

conceptual thinking, Jacobi proposed that we could obtain knowledge of reality through a process of direct intuition, unburdened by concepts which can only relate to one another. Friedrich Schleiermacher also saw the need for a supplement to conceptual knowledge as a means to know reality. This supplemental role he assigned to a form of mystical feeling, which plays the functional role of Jacobi's direct intuition. Johann Herbart proposed another description of ego; he postulated ego as a continually moving "point" at which perceiving and perceived ideas converge, and which conversion is the direct knowledge of reality. And Friedrich Bouterwek proposed a view of reality founded on the priority of activity. He understood the reality of the external world to be a direct product of the fact that we experience resistance when we act.

One would not want to deny the significant differences among these post-Kantian philosophers. Nevertheless, all of these thinkers proceed in two similar ways. First, each advocates along with Fichte and Schelling the notion that practical reason, the expression of freely choosing ego, creates the world. Each argues that an essential connection to reality is possible which is not provided by the conceptual, positive sciences. Second, there begins to emerge in their thinking the idea of process. Ego externalizes itself, as it were, in various ways. In the case of Jacobi, it does so through conceptual thinking and through direct intuition. In the cases of Schelling and Fichte, however, there is an implicit logical, almost temporal, ordering; ego externalizes itself as positive science, and then comes to realize that *it* has all along been the agent of this externalization.

Hegel takes up the process that is implicit in these thinkers and develops it fully. Hegel sees the self-understanding of ego (which he will name *Geist*) not as a direct intuition side by side

with ego's other externalizations, but as the result of a lengthy, elaborate process. At times Hegel seems to suggest that this self-understanding is achieved through broad historical movements which culminate in the world of the modern Germanic people. At other times Hegel seems to suggest that this process is less connected with actual historical events and more of a dialectical play of concepts, in which full self-understanding is achieved as an "internal" process. In both cases, the self-understanding of ego comes to its full conclusion in the thinking of Hegel himself.

In all this Hegel is at great pains to distinguish his thinking sharply from those who would apprehend reality through an act of direct intuition or mystical feeling. He argues that no act of direct intuition, no feeling, or no mystical apprehension can take us to reality. There is but one way to reality and that is through the rigor of conceptual thinking. Kant was wrong; reality *can* be accessed by conceptual thinking. But it is hard work. Hegel argues that his own thinking displays the rigor necessary to come to reality, a rigor marked by what he calls the seriousness of the concept.

However hard the work, Hegel surely must have known that he comes to the same point as all the post-Kantians, including the most romantic among them. For there is only one reason that reality can be accessed by *Geist*/ego and that is because reality is *Geist*/ego's creation in the first place. Hegel transcends the chasm which Kant opened up by means of a dialectical process. The result of this process is achieved at the end, but it has been implicit from the beginning. Kant's world-in-itself is no longer seen negatively (as what is not phenomenal, not knowable, etc.), but as what it is positively and in its essence: it is the non-phenomenal *Geist*/ego externalized and viewed as an (unknowable) object. External reality is the negating power of the ego, reified, or viewed in an

abstracted, alienated manner. The stunning radicalism of not only Hegel's, but of the entire post-Kantian idealist undertaking is suggested in the preface to Hegel's *Phenomenology of Mind*. There, in a formulation that might make Prometheus blush, Hegel contrasts his goal with that of the entire Western tradition of thought that went before him. He voices the hope that philosophy might become science, that it "might be able to relinquish the name of love of knowledge and be actual knowledge – that is what I have resolved to try." Hegel aims to achieve actual knowledge. But what does this mean? For Hegel it means transcending the reified world in which mind/ego misconstrues itself as but one of a number of given beings in the world. It means realizing that what is true is not only substance, but just as much subject.

Hegel uses many different terms to describe the creative/ destructive power which comes to know itself as what is most true. That which knows itself as both substance and subject Hegel calls *Geist*, which is variously translated as "spirit" or "mind." But the internal necessity of the dialectical play by which spirit knows itself fully is predicated upon its creative/destructive power. This power Hegel calls in the *Phenomenology* the power of ego, "the ego or becoming in general." The path by which genuine knowledge is obtained is the path of mediation, a path by which self-identity moves itself, a path which is "the moment of the ego which is for itself, pure negativity or, reduced to its pure abstraction, simple becoming." Hegel refers to the ego as "the power of the negative, or pure actuality." The power of ego is at once creative and destructive. It creates the world we know, including the externality of ego itself. It also dissolves that world through its abstractive power. This ego lies at the heart of Hegel's thought; ego has the power to abstract from all externality, including its own. The power of ego completes

itself when it knows itself as both the world which it has created and as the creator of that world. In this way, the concepts of negativity and actuality – which seem ordinarily to oppose one another – are transcended. Here in the *Phenomenology* the chasm between substance and subject has been bridged:

> When the negative thus appears at first as the non-identity of the ego and its object, it is just as much the non-identity of the substance with itself. What seems to happen outside it, as an activity directed against it, is its own doing; and thus the substance shows that it is essentially subject.

When this occurs, *Geist* has made its existence equal to its essence, and has become an object for itself as it is. With this, "the phenomenology of the spirit is concluded."

We might fairly ask what has been achieved here. After all, as Hegel says, new fields of knowledge will not arise out of this understanding. New fields of knowledge, if they come to exist, will consist of positive knowledge, far inferior to the realization of the unity of subject and substance. Even though achieved only by way of a complex dialectical process, the unity of subject and substance seems to be a one-time aware-ness, the very awareness of which constitutes its whole meaning. There is an abstract, formal character to this kind of knowledge, a knowledge which Hegel elsewhere asserts has transcended formalism. There is a sheer concept-mongering to this knowledge, which Hegel says takes us beyond the conceptualization of the positive sciences. Ultimately, for Hegel these are no objections: "Because, as we put it above, the substance is in itself subject, all content is its own reflection in itself." True knowledge, or *Wissenschaft*, is where ego knows itself as ego and thus actualizes itself in that self-

knowledge. The self-knowledge which heals the breach between subject and substance, between objectivity and subjectivity, does not produce useful new fields of learning about the external world, but is a purely formal conceptual identity. It is akin to discovering at once that your worst enemy and your best friend are not found in others, but that they are you.

Though Hegel asserted the superiority of the ego's self-actualization to the knowledge of the positive sciences, he in no way denied the truth or the utility of the positive sciences or of mathematics. To the contrary, as did Kant and other thoughtful exponents of Kant's insights, Hegel aims to understand and to provide the proper basis or footing for the positive sciences. The post-Kantian idealists advance the notion that our knowledge of the external world is founded upon the relation of concepts to one another. This portion of post-Kantian idealism is really no different from the philosophical positivism of Comte, or Spencer, or their latter day successors. Logical positivistic philosophy of science is in *this* way no different in its understanding than is post-Kantian idealism. Both agree that the kind of knowledge offered by the positive sciences such as chemistry, biology and so forth, is the working out of laws based upon concepts which are the products of our minds. The fundamental insight of idealist philosophy is consistent with modern science, namely, that being and knowledge are thought only in consciousness, as a kind of consciousness. The historical overlay of Hegel and the other post-Kantian idealists may have obscured this relationship. And the existence of higher knowledge for Hegel and the post-Kantian idealists may have misled their critics about how far they travel together. For the post-Kantian idealists root all positive knowledge upon a purpose, upon ways of looking at the external world founded upon the ends or purposes of ego.

Though modern linguistic philosophy has claimed for itself

the mantle of a philosophy consistent with modern science, it is really no such thing. When we ask "what do we mean when we say," such questions may clarify the use and misuse of our words, but they offer no way to look at the world or to explain modern science. Linguistic philosophy flatters itself that it can assist as a "handmaiden" to modern science by "clearing away the intellectual underbrush," but it is as barren as a handmaiden can be. Positive knowledge arises only out of the power of creative thinking about the external world. And this creative thinking is founded upon the power of the idealist philosophy of ego, which advances the priority of practical reason as the foundation of our knowledge.

The philosophy of Descartes and early modern thinkers advances a corrosive individuality - destroying mind, which abstracts from all merely apparent knowledge and penetrates to true knowledge of the external world. The idealism of Schelling, Fichte, Hegel and the post-Kantians offers in its place an individuality-destroying ego. This ego is the creative/ destructive power *per se*, and its essence lacks all unique characteristics save for this power. To the extent that ego has not abstracted itself from all uniqueness such as gender, location, master or slave, and so forth, to that same extent ego has not unified its essence and its existence. It has not yet become what it is most fully, most really, most essentially. To be fair, there is and remains throughout post-Kantian idealism a certain unclarity. At times it seems that the ego as destructive/ creative power cannot and should not be equated with the ego of unique human beings. Similar to gnosticism's "spirit," ego is a pure power which manifests itself finally in and through the whole (the Absolute). Upon this view individual human beings at best express a portion of the entirety of ego which unifies subject and substance. Elsewhere, it seems as if discrete human beings are able to express and thus to actualize the power of

ego to unify subject and substance. Idealist philosophy shuttles between, and in some ways surreptitiously trades upon, these two different accents – though it is perhaps no surprise that ego is invariably understood to complete its activity in the work of the German idealists themselves.

Practical Reason as Will

How are we to comprehend this ego, which is the creative/destructive/abstractive power which creates itself and the entirety of being? After all, this ego cannot be quite like anything else there is, for all other being is its creation. For idealist philosophy, this is indeed just the point: to accord the external world an independent reality, and then to explain ego as some type of being within that reality is to commit the cardinal misunderstanding. It will perhaps occur to the reader that this is precisely the perennial problem which arises when one aims to describe an all-powerful, omniscient creative god. Any and all descriptions drawn from the world which such a god has created inevitably fail to do justice to this god. God stands over and above his creation, and is inadequately able to be comprehended by descriptions drawn from this creation. All one can glean from the creation are perhaps hints, or analogies, according to which god might be pointed to in a rough and ready, but never complete way. Without such hints – which are usually provided in revealed texts – it is impossible to derive a code of ethics or any guidance as to how to worship god or to live a life which pleases god.

One would not be wrong to conclude that that ego of German idealism stands in for what for theologians is called god. As *the* creative/destructive power, ego is responsible for the creation of being, much the way Yahweh creates being in the Torah. At the same time, like Yahweh, ego transcends the being of its creation. Schelling offers a formulation in *The*

Nature of Human Freedom which expresses this perfectly:

> In the final and highest instance there is no other
> Being than will. Will is primordial Being, and
> all predicates apply to it alone – groundlessness,
> eternity, independence of time, self affirmation!
> All philosophy strives only to find this highest
> expression.

The ego of German idealism is like the god of the Hebrew
Bible or of the Christian god; it externalizes itself in its
creation(s), but remains more than its externalizations. How
then are we to comprehend it? How are we to give "content" to
the idea of ego? Like Paul, who tried to fuse together a
"spiritual body," or like Descartes and his successors, who
tried to find a way to explain the interaction of minds and
bodies, German idealism has set for itself a virtually insoluble
problem: how can we comprehend the creative power of ego
through its manifestations? This, after all, was the self-imposed
task of Kant's successors, namely, to take the pure negativity
of Kant's noumenal world and to give it "content."

The answer to this question, limited as it is, lies in the
concept which Schelling described above: ego is will. The
future tense word "will" expresses a want, a desire, a lack. In a
complete, self-sufficient world one supposes there would be no
"will" because there would be no insufficiency, no need for
change, no intent, no future, indeed no time at all. One might
fairly ask whether describing ego as "will" has accomplished
anything, or whether it has simply substituted one inexplicable
word for another. But much has occurred in this move. The ego
of German idealism differs in a fundamental way from the god
of the Hebrew Bible or of Christianity: it is at the same time
both the power to create or externalize and the very externalizations themselves. The ego, or will, of German idealism is a
self-creating power, a power which is both itself and its

creations. There is no gulf between the creator and its creation; as Feuerbach points out at excruciating length, a theological view totally misconstrues the reality of immanence. The world (ego) creates itself; and it is we in turn who create the gods. Although ego understands itself only through the mind, it is the character of ego to externalize itself. The mind is but one way in which ego creates, and perhaps not the most significant one at that. The activity, the impulse, the striving – which is captured in the word "will" – are what constitute the core of ego. Schelling, as we have seen, equates will with being itself. And Fichte also takes this course in identifying ego with infinite striving or infinite doing. It is the infinite striving of ego which creates the world of being. It is true that for Hegel especially, as a professor in his lecture hall, mind is the way in which ego becomes aware of itself in a fully self-conscious manner – and thus achieves the highest self-awareness as *Geist* knowing itself – but this is just as true for the other German idealists. Implicit in their view is the idea that self-awareness is an act of the intellect; but it is equally true for them, as for Hegel, that intellect is but one way in which ego has externalized itself and created the world. Mind may be the crown of ego's self-realization; but it rests upon, and is indeed one expression of a churning, restless, striving, creative ego.

All this allows us to make sense of why German idealism would identify what is most real with "will." Why, for example, would Schopenhauer choose to identify Kant's noumenal world with "*Wille*" rather than "mind" or "spirit" or "intuition?" Why take such a loaded word as "will," coming as it does from everyday human usage, and equate it with true being? Why especially, given that Schopenhauer is at pains to explain that the underlying reality of "Wille" is not exactly equivalent to human willing? The answer is that ego as will is the prevalent thought of German idealism. It is more or less

explicit, as in Schelling, or more or less implicit, as in Hegel – but the idea that what is most real is the striving, creative/destructive power of ego is present at the core of post-Kantian German idealism.

Schopenhauer, of course, is most explicit in describing being as will. In *The World as Will and Representation* (Volume One, Fourth Book), he self-consciously turns upside down the early modern view of knowing and willing:

> Such a view [the early modern view], therefore, regarded the will as of a secondary nature, instead of knowledge, which is really secondary. The will was even regarded as an act of thought, and was identified with the judgment, especially by Descartes and Spinoza...According to the whole of my fundamental view, all this is a reversal of the true relation. The will is first and original; knowledge is merely added to it as an instrument belonging to the phenomenon of the will.

For Schopenhauer, will is equivalent to being, and knowledge is a secondary manifestation of will. Will expresses itself in many ways; what we see as differences in the world of external things (the phenomenal world) are different manifestations of will. Human willing, including through our capacity for knowledge, is but one way in which will expresses itself in the world. The way in which we will is what is unique about human beings.

We can know the rules or patterns or laws according to which the manifestations of will are found in the external world. These are found in the knowledge which comprises modern science, and there is thus for Schopenhauer no incompatibility whatsoever between modern science and the fact that Will and Being are identical. The entirety of the

external world's operations could be known fully, through the relation of cause and effect, and could thus seem to be wholly determined – and this would not invalidate in any way that one's essence as will lies behind this world.

Now it seems at first blush that for Schopenhauer there remains at least one way in which the intellect can achieve some independence from will. It seems that intellect preserves sufficient independence to be able to choose to quiet the will. And for Schopenhauer, when the will or striving is quieted, there lies the best hope to minimize the ever-present suffering of the world's creatures. Yet even this role of the intellect turns out to be derivative. Thinking is but a certain kind of externalization of will, and hence quieting the will is an act of will itself. We call this particular act of willing "self-knowledge." Here theoretical or pure reason is militantly in tow to practical reason. Like the other German idealists, Schopenhauer at times accents the general Wille, and at times its expression in human actions. While it is unlikely that without the experience of human willing anyone would ever have come to the thought that will is primordial Being, this does not disturb Schopenhauer's view that it is will which creates the entire world of representations within which we function every day. Our human character includes that particular type of striving or willing which is thinking, which ironically can bring some surcease to our restless striving.

Let us consider the ground we have traversed. For Heracleitus, character for man is destiny. How a human being is shaped or oriented defines his horizons, his possibilities, his very destiny. The human being is at each and every point of his life a given set of conditions, which are called his character, and this character is his fate. Even for so different a philosophy as Locke's, there is a persisting "me" which is each human being. In his *Essay*, Locke depreciates the idea of soul, arguing that it is the consciousness of a "persisting me" which gives

human beings their essential quality. This "persisting me" Locke calls the "self." This "self" is not being created by an ego at every given moment; to the contrary, the self is a persisting consciousness which is more or less given to each conscious being. As that which persists, we selves are in some way un-free, we are in some way tied to the consciousness which persists within us. What persists for German idealism, however, is nothing which ties us to our specific place and time; what persists is what lies at the base of our being, which is a restless, striving ego which is intrinsically free. This ego or this "I" is what shapes us, and to the extent that we remain shaped by our specificity we are not yet free; we are to this extent not realizing our essential freedom.

It is this understanding which informs the modern view of what it means to be a human being. It is this understanding which gains acceptance in the leading philosophical schools of modernity. This point could be made generally; to illustrate, however, let us consider a school of thought which is often presented as diametrically opposed to German idealism: the American philosophy of pragmatism, explicated most popularly by William James. James and other pragmatists saw themselves standing in fundamental opposition to German idealism. In regard to idealism's usual historical overlay and idealism's view that there is a type of knowledge of reality which transcends the positive sciences, they were surely correct in that understanding. But what is the pragmatic philosopher's understanding of what it means to be a human being? In his *Psychology*, James splits man into the "me" and the "I." In his *Psychology*, James says that the "me" is the entire collection of one's states of conscious-ness and the "I" or ego is the passing "that which is conscious at any given moment." But here is the point: for James it is the "I" or the "ego" which is the creative human force. What is this "I?" James says that the ego is no physical thing, but is itself a

thought. So much for James' alleged opposition to idealism on this point. But even more tellingly, the "I" or ego is not a passive mental construct, but is a thought which "appropriates" certain other thoughts in the past into a "me." For James the "I" or the ego is continually creating the "me;" the "me" is an accretion of ideas that the creative appropriation of the "I" joins together. James' pragmatic philosophy places the core of the human being in the mysterious "I" which has the power to shape its "me." The "I" or ego creates a "me" or a "self" as its context. If it could create its "me" in one way, it could perhaps just as easily create it in some other way.

In like vein Nietzsche – who elsewhere calls the ego or the "I" a superstitious remnant of soul – describes what occurs when memory and ego collide. When memory and pride of ego collide, memory gives way to pride which says, "I could not have acted in such way." The ego or "I" thus creates a new "me" more to its liking, a "me" that suits its desire to be understood in one way and not in another.

To the extent that a "me" lies prior to, or shapes the ego or "I," to this same extent this "me" is a hindrance to the pure creative/destructive power of the ego. Now in many cases in human history, perhaps even in most cases, these limits are what lie precisely in the way; humans are shaped by their time, place, and circumstances, including and especially their own foolish consistencies and their own self-understandings that derive from their specific situation. But this is just the point: for German idealism, for Nietzsche's self-legislating man, for pragmatic philosophy, and for modern thought generally, the goal is to liberate the ego from all such arbitrary, alienated, and self-imposed limits on the freedom of ego to choose. Under the influence of German idealist philosophy we have moved from a world where self-repression is the key to realizing one's humanity, to a world where the key is self-development.

Freedom as Autonomy of the Ego

How is freedom possible for ego, and in what does it consist? To be free is conventionally understood as being able to choose or to act without being determined by what is "outside." What is most free is least determined or shaped by what comes from the outside. This kind of freedom is called by post-Kantian idealists "negative freedom." This is the freedom of early modern political thought, a freedom which is instrumental in its character. Early modern thinkers like Locke promoted the idea of freedom or liberty because it was useful for other human ends. The kind of societies that were relatively free were the kind of societies that promoted the virtues which fulfilled human life, above all the development of mind. Tolerance, for example, was a virtue because it produced a context within which reason could operate and could transcend the arbitrariness of revealed religious dogma. Humans should be free because freedom conduces to the proper understanding of the world; it is the way in which humans exercise their essential quality as minds. So, too, freedom understood in this way conduces to the fullest human ability to employ one's labor upon the fallow world and to make it useful for human purposes. Such freedom, of course, is not unlimited but is always balanced by the other ends which it helps to realize.

Post-Kantian idealists are unified in their criticism of such "negative freedom." Negative freedom is for them limited, partial and inadequate. Negative freedom is inadequate because it sets ego against the external world. Negative freedom is characteristic of a world of strife, wherein ego is estranged both from the material world and from other human egos in that world. That is why it is the hallmark of negative freedom that it must be maintained by compulsion. Negative freedom is the freedom of Hobbes, where each is set against all others in a world which requires eternal vigilance.

Let us be clear. Post-Kantian idealists do not deny that such a world of blind compulsion and order exists. This is the world of modern science. This is the world which is understood, in Hans Vaihinger's phrase, "as if" absolutely every occurrence is fully determined under the sheerest necessity of cause and effect. Modern science continues to build out our capacity to understand the operation of an external, phenomenal world and to make us more effective in that world. This includes the scientific study of human beings as well. The more science learns, the more human behavior seems to fall under the sway of determination and law-like necessity. And the more we are thus able to manipulate human behavior through chemical, biological and genetic treatments. No subject is or can be off limits to such inquiry, and there is in principle no bound to such knowledge. We could in principle account for every single human choice and every single human action.

But the concepts of compulsion and order by which we understand the external world are the creations of ego itself. For this reason, no matter how fully science might account for the operations of the external world, there remains behind this world, as it were, the irreducible essence of ego in which our deepest and truest being resides. The creation of ego which we call modern science is itself of only instrumental value, in so far as it creates for us ever more efficient means to achieve our ends. But *whose* ends are these? They are the ends of ego, and if ego were bound or constricted in some way, it would be in just *that* way unable to use scientific thought to shape its ends and to re-make the world. Modern science only seems to dissolve everything into matter in motion. But who or what is doing the dissolving? Whose ends does such dissolution promote? What is the purpose of modern science as an enterprise? A scientist might flatter himself and say that it is to promote human welfare. But that depends on how this

knowledge is utilized. Knowledge can produce nuclear power or nuclear weapons, life-saving devices or biological weapons. Science is purely instrumental; the world it dissolves and re-makes is fully in the service of – ego. Though science seems to reduce the world of freedom to nothingness, ironically ego becomes all the more powerful as the transformative power of that very world.

What could possibly shape or guide – or for that matter, inhibit – the choices of an ego which lies behind the phenom-enal world? What does the radical freedom of ego really mean? If ego or "I" is essentially a thought which willfully appro-priates other thoughts, from what is this ego free? It must be free from all that is not ego. It must act only in and for itself, determined in no way by what is "outside" ego. Such an ego must be free not only of the external material world, and of other humans and their desires, but also of its own body, its own location, and its own history, including even the immediately prior thought or choice of ego itself. If ego were shaped by its prior choices, the "me" would shape the "I;" but as we have seen, it is the "I" that creates the "me."

Ego must act out of itself. When it acts out of itself, it unifies its existence and its essence. When it does so, it surpasses mere negative freedom and achieves "positive freedom." True or positive freedom is found when ego realizes that it has created the world; this world is its world. This positive freedom Schelling calls "the one and all of philo-sophy." This is the freedom which Hegel extols in his *Philosophy of History* when he says that "the history of the world is none other than the progress of the consciousness of freedom." Freedom is achieved only when ego understands that the world of being does not stand outside as some estranged entity, but is in fact its own creation. Hegel says in the

Encyclopedia, "freedom is only present where there is no other for me, which is not myself."

What does this radical freedom look like when it is exercised? If there is nothing outside ego, including the prior choices of ego, that can guide its choices, where does ego find the raw material, as it were, in order to choose? To where does ego repair when it seeks to choose? What does it mean for ego to act out of itself? Such a standard of self-legislation is customarily referred to as "autonomy," and German idealists and their successors use this term freely. As Habermas says in *Knowledge and Human Interests* in commenting on Fichte, "Only the ego that apprehends itself in intellectual intuition as the self-pointing subject obtains autonomy." Here we enter into difficult terrain. The goal of ego, in which ego unifies its essence and existence, is to be "autonomous." But the literal meaning of autonomy (auto-nomy) is to give laws to oneself, and we have seen that Kant argued if a choice is to be genuinely free, and not merely random or spontaneous, it must derive from a law-like necessity. For Kant, we must act out of an inner necessity if we are to avoid being determined by external necessity.

Kant's successors follow him in the idea that there is a necessity to the acts of ego's free expression. Ego is the noumenal world understood as a pure creation, beyond the antinomy of necessity and freedom. When ego acts, its acts both freely and as it must. Here post-Kantian idealism comes up against the same insoluable problem as any theological conception of an omnipotent, self-sufficient god. What would such a god do? Why would such a god "do" anything at all? Why would such a god not rest within his self-sufficiency, if he is indeed self-sufficient? Why would a self-sufficient god choose to create the world? Nevertheless, here is the world and here we are within it. But why? All attempts to answer this

question inevitably offer pale and unconvincing reasons why a god might have created this world, based upon analogies to human motivation. Perhaps god was bored; perhaps he wished to be worshipped; perhaps he wished to be amused. We are lost in the fog of mystery from which can emerge no persuasive conclusion.

So it is for the freely choosing ego of idealist philosophy. What is it that that ego should be moved to do, and why? Why does ego create the world of being which it does? Here, too, all one can say is that there must be some intrinsic necessity to it, but if there is, it is a necessity which passes all human under-standing. A theologian might assert that the unity of god's essence and existence required the world to be created just as it is – though be unable even to hint at why this is so. An idealist philosopher might assert that the unity of ego's essence and existence requires it to externalize itself just as it does – though be unable to hint at why this is so.

Here idealist philosophy aims to overcome its emptiness in two related, but completely unjustified ways. First, it can fairly argue that ego stands beyond the antinomy of freedom and necessity, that ego acting out of the unity of its essence and existence is beyond the either/or of freedom or necessity. But then to proceed to make the hallmark of ego's activity and the intrinsic goal of its entire project "freedom" is more than perverse. It is altogether to trade on the everyday use of the word "freedom" in a context in which it can have no such meaning. Having done that, idealist philosophy then aims to return to the everyday world and give some content to its conception of positive freedom – a step which seems contra-dictory on its face, if ego stands behind and beyond the phenomenal world altogether. Hegel, for example, aims to give content to the notion of positive freedom in his *Philosophy of Right*. For Hegel the "freely" choosing ego points to subsuming

individual human egos in the broader entity which is the modern state. Here individual egos are reconciled with one another in a larger whole, because they understand that they are not set against one another, but somehow find their fulfillment in their role in the whole. Hegel's archenemy Schopenhauer offers a less political view, but one quite analogous nevertheless. For Schopenhauer, Will is best served when each of its manifestations (each human being, for example) sees that he or she is but one manifestation of the single unceasing Will. They break through the veil of Maya and see that they are not set against other manifestations of Will, but are like them, and in this realization quiet their striving and cease their conflict with other manifestations of Will. These formulations all trade on the familiarity of ego, spirit, and will. We are not gods, but we are egos, spirits, or wills, and we seem to have a kind of direct intuition of these faculties. These everyday, understandable human faculties are given a "transcendental," noumenal character – as Absolute Spirit, as Will, and so forth – and from these in turn are derived specific human faculties. But it remains unclear, to be polite about it, how renaming god as ego, spirit, or will clarifies anything about the way in which such an entity might choose to externalize itself.

The difficulty for all such accounts – Schelling's, Fichte's, Hegel's, or Schopenhauer's – is that freely creating ego does not and cannot point persuasively to any particular choice or outcome. Having made freedom ego's highest – indeed, its only – end, there is no place to turn to find guidance for its choices. Abstractly, it may stand beyond the antinomy of freedom and necessity, but practically it neither can nor does point anywhere at all. Negative freedom may well be partial and incomplete, but so-called positive freedom is completely empty. Having excluded every external basis for guiding ego's choices – because these would limit its freedom and

misconstrue its essence – ego is left with no standard what-soever for its choices. Ego is free, but free to do what? Freely choosing ego points to no way of life. Freely choosing ego opens up the world in a new and bizarre way. If ego cannot mirror its choices upon an order found in the cosmos, how will it choose to orient itself? Upon what basis will it legislate for itself? How will it exercise its freedom? Freedom is no longer important instrumentally, to secure other human ends. Freedom is intrinsically important because it is the highest human end. It is not and cannot be important what one chooses; what is important is that one chooses.

Authenticity as Moral Life

Upon such a view, how is it possible to lead an ethical or moral life? In what could ethics or morality consist? We find that when ego creates knowledge by looking at the phenomenal world scientifically, it is ego which shapes what we find to be important or valuable. It is ego that creates the pragmatic standard for what will count as knowledge. And when it does, the knowledge which it creates is unable in turn to give direction to ego.

Let us consider briefly the major ways in which the contemporary secular world seeks to understand human behavior and action. These consist mainly in the social sciences – in political science, economics, and sociology; in psychology; and in philosophy. Each of these fields aims in its own way to build out our knowledge of humanity. Each aims to provide accounts of how humans act, along the particular dimension or sets of concerns which it addresses. Each aims to establish and to clarify connections between patterns of behavior and choices, with the goal of explaining and ultimately predicting aspects of human behavior. But what guidance can be drawn from these fields?

In the case of political science, which studies the institutions of government, the effort is made to categorize types of government or governmental institutions and to clarify what inputs and outputs are typical of each. But to what end? Political scientists are able to clarify outcomes implicit in various choices – liberal democracies will tend to produce certain kinds of outcomes, tyrannies others, and so forth. They are able to clarify patterns within certain types of governmental orders as well – how political parties function, what motivates voters, and so forth. But they are unable to draw from this study any conclusion about what kind of political order ego should prefer. The knowledge of political science is instrumental through and through; if one seeks a certain end, here is how to achieve it, here is what to avoid. But it cannot speak to the prior choices of the end itself.

When it does try, as in the case of modern political philosophers, its conclusions are inevitably unpersuasive. The core of such philosophical efforts usually focuses around the idea that – often following Kant – one or several popular virtues can be deduced from an analysis of political life. The usual candidate is the virtue of tolerance. But the political doctrine of tolerance arose out of the view that humans are essentially mind, not ego. As mind, humans require certain conditions best and most fully to exercise their minds. Among these conditions is tolerance, for tolerance permits inquiry and debate and this allows humans to exercise their essential character as mind. The conclusion that humans understood as essentially freely choosing ego, however, should favor tolerance is the sheerest prejudice. This is simply to import into one's analysis a current prejudice of liberal democracy, without any theoretical foundation whatsoever. Anything which constrains ego, including the beliefs of others, reflects ego which has not yet realized its essence to will freely. One might choose to tolerate

the views of others; but as ego, one could with equal justification ignore, or utterly crush, the views of others.

This can be observed most clearly in the work of John Rawls, perhaps the most widely admired and significant contemporary political philosopher. Rawls aims to justify certain minimal political virtues. This he does in the spirit of modern idealist philosophy, by stripping away each and every "accidental" condition of humans, that is, gender, economic status, and so forth. He aims to abstract from humans' actual positions and to repair to an "initial position" in which humans lack all specificity. But in so reducing humans to sheer willing ego, he undermines the basis for preferring one choice to another. In *Giants and Dwarfs* Allan Bloom focuses on the core problem of Rawls' thought: "the self is prior to the ends which are affirmed by it." The self, or what we have here referred to as ego, cannot be guided by any external master, for it creates its own ends.

Contemporary economists put a different set of questions to the external world. They seek to clarify patterns which exist between the supply and demand for goods and services, including the abstract commodity of money. Economists seek to discover patterns between different economic systems and their likely outcomes. They are able to clarify patterns within economic systems as well – how increasing the supply of money affects prices, how competition affects prices, and so forth. But they are unable to draw from this study any conclusion about what kind of economic system or institutions ego should prefer. The knowledge provided by economics is instrumental through and through; if one seeks certain ends, here is how one is more likely to achieve them, here is how they are more likely to be frustrated. But it cannot speak to the prior choice of an end itself. When it does try, its conclusions are as unpersuasive as those of political science, and for the

very same reason. For example, economists largely agree that some limited set of choices will benefit the whole, and will increase the net benefit to the sum of utility functions which is the entire economy. In this vein, economists have largely supported the notion (through perhaps less so in recent years) that free trade will benefit an economy, on the whole. But to find guidance here one must presuppose that it is good to benefit the whole at the expense of some, and economics can offer no reason why that should be so. Indeed, economics cannot say why one or a small number of individuals should not benefit at the expense of everyone else. This, as any novice legislator knows, is the political problem of trade policy.

A narrower, and less useful but seemingly stronger case, has been advanced in optimization theory. If a decision will benefit at least some people, and no one will lose, this would seem to be unambiguously good. However rare this might be in practice, at least this kind of decision might offer guidance to freely choosing egos whose existence lies prior to their choices. But this, too, merely presupposes, and for no good reason, that egos seek to choose what is in any way "good" or beneficial for someone else. Why should egos care? Perhaps egos might choose to take pleasure in the suffering of other egos, or at least in self-flattering comparisons with them. Unless one assumes from the outset some kind of utilitarian moral sentiment, economics cannot and will not be able to offer any but instrumental guidance to freely choosing ego.

Contemporary sociology (and anthropology) approaches the human world in yet another way. Contemporary sociology aims to clarify the patterns between different kinds of social groups – families, social classes, communities, tribes, and so forth – and the kinds of human behavior which result. It aims to clarify the relationships between differing social groupings or institutions and patterns of human behavior. Like modern political science

and economics, sociology in this way produces only instrumental knowledge for freely choosing egos. But behind the current practice of sociology lies a somewhat more honest, if not more successful approach. For implicit in the practice of contemporary sociology is the aim everywhere to expose the arbitrary social limitations on freely choosing ego. Sociologists aim more straightforwardly than their other social scientific brethren to free the world of social institutions from their reified, thing-like objectivity. Sociology looks at social institutions as arbitrary creations which shape and limit the expression of human ego. The task of modern sociologists is a task of liberation. Today, this enterprise is a bit like aiming to free a prisoner who escaped long ago. Is it not the case that our social institutions, all of nature, and the gods themselves have long since been understood to be part of the "standing reserve" which is present to be manipulated by human ego? Do not all social institutions have an apparent arbitrariness today? Are they not all viewed as institutions which lack a rational foundation and which reflect "ideologies" that serve only to justify one or another arbitrary arrangement? How reified, or natural, could the social order possibly appear today – at a time when humans have the capacity to re-configure their environment; of aiming to democratize the entire world; of replaceable institutions and replaceable body parts; of gene splicing, cloning and the ability to re-create human life; and of the ever-present background belief that humans have it within our power to destroy the whole world? Surely, as anyone who has ever taught a college freshman knows, the problem today is not that the social order is too reified. Today's social order is a contingent social order, supported only by the gossamer film of ideology, pure and simple.

The field of psychology approaches external reality in yet another way. It aims to clarify patterns or relationships between

stimuli and responses. It aims to clarify the ways in which the behavior of individual human beings can be understood as instances of broader patterns, and ultimately predicted. In its purest scientific form, in the field of neuro-psychology and other forms of behavioralism, it studies the workings of the human brain and the connections between the way in which the brain works and what we customarily call human behavior. It provides instrumental knowledge, pure and simple. It does not and cannot provide knowledge or guidance about how we should act, but at best patterns of how we do act. It aims to provide knowledge that permits the manipulation of the human brain or of human behavior, but cannot say whether or why some outcomes are preferable to others. Behavioral psychology treats human behavior, or the human brain in the same way any other science treats its "portion" or "slant" on external reality. It does not aim to go "behind" human behavior, as it were, and to treat it from the inside. The psyche which psych-ology investigates has no more or less status than any other portion of external reality. It treats its subject matter with all the formality of any other science.

Where certain types of psychology do aim to go beyond this formal, positive knowledge, they too aim to achieve the liberation of human ego. Freud, the founder of modern psychology, creates a conceptual framework according to which to understand human beings. For Freud, behind all human choices lies a blind, restless power of willing which he calls "it" (id). This energy can be channeled by the "I" (ego). Though it is Freud's deeply held view that there is more to psychic life than exists in either latent or actual consciousness, it is nevertheless the case that "ego" is the only point at which awareness of the external world can open up to consciousness. Though Freud divides the restless willing of "id" from the pure choosing of "ego," it is through the choices of ego that humans

become what they can most fully be. And how does this happen? It happens when ego is liberated from the bondage of unknown forces and limitations which arise out of the specific circumstances of one's life. And what is the point, or the "end" of psychoanalysis? It is to free ego from such external compulsion; it is to allow ego to choose more "freely." It is to release ego from the grip of blind determination by the forces of one's family life, the events and incidents one has experienced, one's traumas, and so forth. When ego brings these unknown forces to consciousness, ego thereby frees itself from their power. Ego is then able to choose freely. But what should such ego choose? This cannot be said. It is free, but free to do what?

Contemporary humanistic psychology follows Freud in this regard: it sees its task as the liberation of ego from the constraints of the external world. This is not accomplished by finding one's place in one's group, nor in directing oneself through reason, nor in choosing god, nor in perfecting our ability to know the laws according to which the cosmos operates. Rather, we find it in freeing ourselves from the constraints of the external world in order to become who we are most fully. This is called a process of self-actualization. Many psychologists such as Carl Rogers speak of self-actualizing tendencies, but the clearest and best exponent of this view is Abraham Maslow. Maslow says that self-actualizing behavior is "the desire to become more and more what one is, to become everything that one is capable of becoming." But we are surely capable of becoming many kinds of persons, including saints or mass murderers. How to choose? Maslow cannot and will not choose. He offers examples of self-actualizing individuals who choose to orient their lives around the search for knowledge, for world peace, or service to god. He offers no examples of individuals who seek

to actualize themselves by conquering the world or by imposing brutal tyrannies – though he might well have. The most Maslow can say is that we self-actualize ourselves by stripping away the determinants of the external world which shape our behavior – until at last ego is acting out of its own motivation. For Maslow there is a hierarchy of human needs and wants which culminate in the highest, most human level of self-actualization. He describes the conclusion of this process: "we become much more free of other people, which in turn means that we become much more ourselves, our Real Selves... our authentic selves, our real identity." In this formulation is revealed the pervasive role of German idealist philosophy at the heart of modernity.

Our humanity is realized most fully in the freely choosing ego, free from all that can and does determine it in the external world. But what should the freely choosing ego choose? The psychologist Wilhelm Reich is admittedly outside the pale of mainstream psychology in many respects. But he could be speaking for mainstream contemporary psychology when he suggests that the human personality is built around points of estrangement that our ego has not "digested" properly. He says: "What we take to be so real, our *selves*, is constructed out of a reaction against just what we do not wish to acknowledge." Our very personalities – that which persists in us – are thus intrinsically dysfunctional, built up out of the arbitrary, accidental, chaotic and determinative external world which surround us. The task, of course, is to teach ego how to "digest" these qualities and hence to liberate ego from them.

In a most revealing passage in *The Drama of the Gifted Child*, the psychologist Alice Miller says: "We cathect an object narcissistically...when we experience it not as the center of its own activity, but as part of ourselves." This is surely well said – and could stand as the very definition of contemporary

thought, which treats the whole of the external world as if it had no independent being, but is the creation and plaything of our own egos. This is the world of "standing reserve," in which all that exists, exists of us, by us, and for us. A member of an ancient tribe might fairly conclude that the entirety of contemporary society suffers from one massive narcissistic disorder.

What can we learn to guide the choices of ego from modern philosophy? Let us leave aside logic, word analysis, epistemeology, the history of philosophy and other sub-fields, and focus on the two disciplines of modern philosophy which aim to provide such guidance. The first is "ethics," a field which is taught in virtually every modern philosophy department. What is taught in "ethics?" One point is certain: contemporary ethical philosophy does not teach an ethos or a way of life. It does not, because it cannot. It cannot, because any and all commands given to ego are restrictions upon ego, and need accordingly to be overcome. Ego cannot say "be loyal to your tribe" or "be a good citizen," for one's membership in a tribe or a political order is not where ego finds its highest expression, namely, freedom. So far from defining one, one's citizenship is but one of many happenstance accidents of one's life, no one of which speaks to the essential freedom of ego. For this reason, ego can find no guidance in the longstanding concept of "honor," which in so many ways has informed much of Western practice. Honor supposes there is something vital or essential about one's station as a member of the group, of one's birth, of one's social class, or of one's country. From this standpoint flow the duties of one's station. But for humans understood essentially as ego, these stations of life are not intrinsic to one's being. To the contrary, they are accidental limitations that stand (falsely) in the path of freely choosing ego. These stations are a shifting concatenation of more or less happenstance qualities; they are

roles, or masks, or possibilities. Honor is the province of a man who acts at odds with the preservation of his life. Dying for one's country, after all, forecloses all future options, in this world at least. Duty is the assignment that grows out of understanding oneself to be a specific kind of person, a person who does or does not engage in certain kinds of activities. Duty arises from an understanding that one occupies a certain position or station which shapes what is meaningful. And the idea of a fixed "position" is precisely what is impossible for ego to accept. Duty, honor, country: these suppose an understanding that ego is somehow defined as a citizen, as a member of a group, or as a member of a social class. But any such determination only binds or restrains a freely choosing ego.

For humans understood as freely choosing ego, the station(s) of life in which one finds oneself are not essential, but accidental. One's ego is not one's citizenship, one's ethnicity, one's gender or any other specific (limiting) quality of one's life. At one's core one is not an American, a husband, a father, or anything else – though one may happen to be all of these. One is not these qualities; these qualities are "roles" which we act out. Roles are parts played by actors, but are not the actors themselves. Who then is the actor? The actor is what Nietzsche calls the "ego superstition," which lies behind each of the roles it plays. There is no guidance which ego can draw from the roles it plays; it might have chosen a different set of roles to act out altogether. Ego realizes its essence not by understanding itself through the roles it plays, but by overcoming them in order to comprehend its freedom.

What can ethical instruction teach to a classroom of such egos? Contemporary ethical philosophy teaches the "clarification of values." Ethicists teach the "ethical aspect," the "ethical component," or the "ethical dimension" of decision-making. It would be difficult to imagine a weaker or more

palpably useless exercise. So-called ethical teachings either import without justification pre-existing preferences (no doubt mirroring politically correct prejudices) or they multiply *ad nauseam* factors and considerations surrounding differing choices. In no event is there any reason to hope that such considerations will actually lead people to behave more ethically.[*] Having foresworn any chance of rooting ethics in habit or convention or the commands of the gods, where can "values clarification" turn to offer guidance? It can offer only instrumental guidance, aiming to root choices somehow in "deeper" values which one holds. But those so-called deeper values are probably only conventional notions of right and wrong, and it would be more honest simply to teach these notions in the first place.

The other field of modern philosophy which proposes guidance for the choices of ego is existentialism. This philosophy, in its numerous forms, holds as a badge of honor that it aims to be fully honest. It seeks to face resolutely and forthrightly the fact that ego cannot find its essence as one kind of being within the external world, but must achieve it by acting out of itself. Such action is referred to as "authentic,' and existentialism aims to make a virtue of this necessity. "Authentic" choices are choices in which ego does not rely on the crutch of other-determinism, but chooses freely out of itself. An authentic choice is one made free of any determination by what is outside. An authentic choice is an uncoerced choice. This places the core of morality in a militantly anti-consequentialist process by which choices are made, not in the actual substantive choices themselves. What

---

[*] In discussing Harvard's ethics curriculum, Harvey Mansfield says in the *Claremont Review of Books*: "There was not much confidence that more reasoning would make you more moral; the hope, I believe, was that reasoning might make you more civil, or at least more deliberate, more cautious..."

would such choices look like? If ego sets all "external" considerations to the side, upon what basis can it choose? An authentic choice is a free choice, but ego might freely choose anything. Authenticity is empty.

The reality of this emptiness is reflected in our common usage of words. There is a saying in colloquial English that a person "has soul." This suggests a certain depth, a humanity, an attunement to something larger than the person so described. There is no conventional counterpart for ego. We do not say a person "has ego." This would point nowhere at all. Indeed, when we say that someone "has a big ego," this points only to the ego's infatuation with itself. In this regard, existentialism is less a philosophy than an attitude. It is an orientation toward the world, an orientation that might best be described as bravado in the face of fate. It is Nietzsche's courage to posit values cheerfully. It is Max Weber's resolution to posit values manfully and intentionally. It is the stance of every existentialist to serve as the presumptive guarantor for one's own decisions in a world into which we have been "thrown" without our consent.

In each of these fields of contemporary thought – and in countless daily popular derivations as well – we find that substantive moral guidance cannot be found for the choices of ego. Everywhere substance gives way to process or method, to the point where process itself becomes the arbiter; what is processed correctly is what is "authentic." Anything can become anything else, depending upon the choice of ego. Energy could be mass; good men could be mass murderers, and so long as this is so "authentically," it is all the same. Nothing is fixed; all is a shifting set of relationships, coming and going according to the being which is granted to it by ego. Such regularity and predictability as we find in the world are put there by ego itself, when ego decides to look at the world under

the aegis of regularity for whatsoever purposes it might have. Such regularity and predictability is misconstrued as "given" to ego when ego has not yet realized its essence. When it does realize its essence, ego not only transforms the world through its externalization, but it understands that it is the creator of being itself.

As ego realizes its self-knowledge as the creator of being, it is able to shape the external world, including human beings, ever more fully. But there is an irony here. As the scientific instruments of ego grow strong, the ego which manipulates them dissolves into pure empty willing. This ego – this X – which grants being to all there is, turns out to be no unique entity itself, but pure blind choosing. Ego does not achieve the quintessence of uniqueness; to the contrary, uniqueness derives only from the accidents of space and time and history through which ego expresses itself. The effort to locate what is most human in ego obliterates humanity in any sense in which we actually experience it. Ego stands as a kind of limiting condition.

The more powerful ego becomes, the more empty ego becomes. The essence of humanity understood as ego is nothing really human at all. This thought surely lay behind the recognition of Meister Eckhart, who saw that the more we act out of ego, the less unique we are as human beings.

SIX

CREDO:

ON HOW TO LIVE

The truth is the more ourselves we are,
the less ego is in us.

Meister Eckhart,
The Tales of Instruction

CREDO:

ON HOW TO LIVE

What might we conclude about these ways in which human being has been understood? The teachings of the Torah root the essence of being human in one's membership in the tribe that worships Yahweh. Individuals are differentiated from one another by their function within the tribe, as priests, warriors, and so forth. But for each member, no matter what his function, one's essential humanity is found through membership in the tribe. This participation points to the way in which human life is best and most fully lived, that is, in obedience to Yahweh.

This view, though possessing the virtues of rooting individuals in a broader social order and pointing to a preferred way of life, omits certain fundamental considerations. Most importantly, it omits any consideration of whether the doctrines relating to Yahweh are in fact true, that is, that the teachings of Moses are genuine revelations of Yahweh, and how we might fairly be able to judge this. In asserting the truth of these claims – and in hinting at a rough and ready pragmatic justification of these claims – the Torah adopts a standpoint which assumes, rather than questions, the truth of its claims. In turn, this leaves open to question whether obedience to Yahweh is indeed the best and most fully human life. Finally, the teachings of Moses do not point beyond themselves toward serious reflection about what might lie before or after one's earthly life.

The Greek idea of soul is a marvelous corrective, one which opens out human being beyond one's tribe to a different relationship with nature, humanity, and the gods. In its purest

Platonic expression, it raises compelling questions to anyone
willing to consider them. At the same time, the Greek notion of
soul, in its various expositions, points to a preferred way of
life, a way of life in which soul exercises its capabilities most
fully. This life has been variously described, but in the main
points toward the full utilization of soul's capacities
culminating in the capacity to think and thus to overcome to
the fullest extent humanly possible the limitations of soul's
association with its body.

Hebrew and Greek strains of thought were melded together
in historic church Christianity. Christian doctrine advances the
notion that human beings are both body and soul, consistent
with Greek doctrine, but fused together in one permanent
psycho-somatic being. This persisting psychosomatic being can
turn toward or away from god, consistent with Hebrew
doctrine. An explicit degree of freedom is supposed here, a
freedom which derives from the church doctrine of soul. The
god to which a Christian turns, however, is not a god whose
doctrines are intended for a specific tribe, but potentially for all
human beings. This doctrine, too, points human beings toward
the best and fullest way of life, the way in which the entire
human being is turned toward God.

Early modern thought breaks apart the psychosomatic
being of Christianity, in favor of a radical separation between
mind and body. Unlike the Greek view, in which soul
expresses itself through body in multiple ways, early modern
thought sharply sunders body from mind, which expresses
itself through its own operations. To be human is to be mind,
and it may be a fact, but it is no decisive fact, that minds seem
invariably to be co-located with bodies. Human beings express
the fullness of their being in the operations of mind, and
through the operation of mind humans can outwit and to some
extent overcome the limitations imposed by bodies – including

our own – in the external world. Mind can do this because of a happy parallelism between the way in which our minds combine ideas and the underlying ideal order of the processes of the external world. To free mind to penetrate to the knowledge of the processes of the external world is the highest way of life, the way of life in which humans find dignity.

Each of these views expresses a way of life that has actually been lived by human beings and which has informed their self-understanding. In locating what is essential about human beings in some quality or qualities which point beyond their everyday expression, each of these views is able to describe a way in which human life is best lived.

But as we have seen, the happy parallelism between mind and the external world of early modern thought was not fated to last. The intellectual power of modern idealism sucks everything into its vortex; the collapse of the parallel worlds of mind and the external world – namely, that the external world is an alienated creation of will – places the freely creative ego at the center of the world. This ego finds expression in such otherwise disparate views as German idealism, the Nietzschean will to power, and various currents of pragmatism. Through these channels it suffuses the whole of contemporary sociology, economics, political science, psychology, and existential philosophy. The freely creative ego comes at us from every direction in today's world, from arcane philosophical expositions to the flat and generally unilluminating work of the social sciences to the slogans of popular culture.

This view opens out human being beyond the expositions which root humanity in a particular essential characteristic. Indeed, it is the underlying intention of this view to transcend all narrow, one-sided essentialist descriptions of what it means to be human. To be human is to be ego; but the essence of ego is openness. Human beings are thus the open beings. Ego lies

behind all accidents of space and time, as the agent of choosing. Ego's essence is not defined by the choices it makes, but by its ability to choose.

But is human being really understood correctly as pure openness or freedom? For as human beings, we do not confront radical openness or freedom. This is not our experience and we are neither misled nor inauthentic in denying that we are fully free to choose at every turn. Our position in space and time, that is, our body, does limit our possibilities. Beyond our bodies, our political and social settings limit the fullness of our possibilities. And as we age, we learn that however free we are, our past is no longer free. We can tell ourselves stories about our past and, as Nietzsche says, suppress or amend our past in our memory. But there is a record of consequences that flows from our prior choices. And it is nowhere clear why those consequences – which are one boundary of what is possible for us – should be of less significance in defining us than what remains our (seeming) openness toward the future. Indeed, perhaps the future only seems more open than the past.

A life in which ego were free to "start over" or be free at every moment would not look like any version of human freedom at all. Complete freedom of the ego would look rather more like the absence of short-term memory, in which every day is a brand new day. Where there is no remembrance of yesterday and its hopes and plans and commitments, this might seem at first inspection to open today to a fullness of possibilities. But our freedom to act is truncated and sharply restricted by the loss of memory which carries us forward over time and binds us to established courses of action. Without the consciousness of persisting identity our choices are narrowed, not opened out. An animal has a less clear sense of persisting identity than a human being – but its choices are narrower, too. And a stone, which we suppose to have no sense of persisting

identity, seems to have no range of choices at all. A stone is not bound by remembrance, mental rules, or sociopolitical structures which orient or shape or limit its "behavior" at each moment. Should we then look upon a stone as a being with an extraordinary capacity to keep its options open? We could suppose that a stone is a being which is so complete in itself that it is (forever) waiting to act. Meanwhile, it is buffeted about, worn down, ground up and otherwise moved about by forces entirely external to it.

Genuine openness to a range of action – what we call "freedom" – requires a consciousness of persisting identity. But paradoxically, this identity is a foundational restriction on the pure freedom of ego. Having an identity means being unable fundamentally to transform that identity. To transcend our persisting identity would sharply limit our choices. We require the relative solidity of our own self-consciousness in order to comprehend and to operate in the external world. Without self-consciousness, or a sense of persisting identity, no comprehension of the external world is possible. Without a persisting sense of identity, the kinds of projects which actually transform the world are not possible. No buildings are constructed, no piano concertos played, and no scientific discoveries made – each of which requires ongoing, persisting identity in order to be carried out. The external world cannot be revealed in its being except to a persisting identity, found in self-consciousness. Without a persisting sense of self-consciousness, there is no comprehension of the external world of nature, of political life, or of the gods. And vice versa: without comprehension of the external world, including our sociopolitical setting, there is but a narrow and limited comprehension of our persisting identity. Perfect "freedom" and openness would be at once the abolition of the capability to recognize any and all beings in the world, oneself included.

Pure freedom is a chimera, unavailable to and inappropriate to human being. What then is this human being, and how can we be described adequately? Are we thrown back to one-sided, essentialist descriptions which are too restrictive to capture the fullness of what it means to be human? We compute and we produce computers, but for all of that we are not essentially computing machines. We are symbol creators, but for all of that we are not essentially symbol creators. We work, but for all of that we are not essentially *homo faber*. We play, but for all of that we are not essentially *homo ludens*. We worship gods, but for all of that we are not essentially theological beings. We carry within ourselves genetic programs, but we are not for all of that essentially selfish genes.

Each of these descriptions emphasizes one facet or aspect of being human. Each can produce interesting theoretical insights and powerful practical consequences. Human beings who act out of one or another of these self-understandings can accomplish feats of piety, sacrifice, self-discipline, and mental creativity. We might say that we are essentially an en-souled being, or a mind, or a collection of chemical elements – and we might discover interesting insights about ourselves and about how to shape ourselves and the world. We could live out our entire life under one or another of these self-understandings, as indeed many people have so lived. But in elevating to our essential nature one of many human capacities, we seem to have lost something of the fullness of what it means to be human.

Humans may well be what we think and do, but we think and do many different things. We think, we work, we play, we worship, we create symbols, we compute, we eat, and so forth. Where is the warrant for elevating one of these capabilities to the level of what or who we really or essentially are? To be pointed, among our many activities human beings create bath

tubs. But for all of that we are neither essentially bath tubs nor bath tub creators. Are we not then driven back to the idea that humans are the fully open beings?

Beavers build dams. We do not think therefore that beavers are dams. Nevertheless, we think of beavers as, among other things, dam builders and not as cave dwellers or flyers. So, too, with human beings. Karl Marx famously said that "all history is nothing but a continuous transformation of human nature." It may well be that human beings have externalized themselves in different ways throughout history. But what is the "human nature" which is the "it" which is continuously transforming itself? Human beings may well be quite open – but a fully open being, with no being but its openness, would not be a human being at all.

Indeed, a fully free and open being, whose essence consists of just that freedom or openness, would be no specific kind of being at all. Any such being would be the "ground" or reason or cause why everything in the world is as it is and not otherwise. This is surely the conclusion of those thoughtful writers who ascribe this freedom to God, who they understand therefore as the ground or cause of all being. So, too, with the German idealist philosophers who ascribe this freedom not to a distant, transcendent God, but to the immanent power of ego or spirit realizing itself through its own activities.

If the essence of human being is pure freedom, by virtue of that freedom we make all else to be as it is; without human being, being as such could not be revealed and would remain mired in formless obscurity. But what kind of "freedom' is this? Post-Kantian idealists suggest that ego or spirit which understands itself transcends the antinomy of freedom and necessity. No longer is freedom set against necessity, but any action of such a being is *both* free and necessary, or in some way neither free nor necessary. But what is the warrant for

taking one of the terms of the antinomy, namely freedom, and elevating that to the essence of all that is? This is at best a misleading use of words.

We are unable to know anything about a fully transcendent God. No more can we know anything about what the resolution of the antinomy of freedom and necessity – if indeed there is one – looks like. To ascribe to it the essential character of freedom – or any other quality – is surely without justification. Indeed, perfect freedom would seem to lack any characteristic we customarily associate with "mind." Perfect freedom would be commensurate with absolute mindlessness. Such perfect freedom would be the freedom of a god who is fully self-sufficient in its own being and thus with no need to will or to externalize itself in any way. Perfect freedom is as likely as not to result in absolutely no activity whatsoever.

But this does not look at all like a human being, who is somehow able to transform the entire world. Human beings are beings who can know ourselves and the external world in many ways. But in doing so, we must know ourselves as persisting consciousness and therefore not as fully free beings. Our comprehension of the external world, in one way or another, is necessary to a persisting sense of self. Our finitude is what allows whatever comprehension of ourselves and of the external world is possible.

We come to know ourselves and we come to know the external world together. Each is the condition for the possibility of the other. This much is fair enough. But from this, modern idealism massively – and wrongly – concludes that we *create* the external world by how we choose to know it. The core of this is captured in the audacity of Hegel's claim to move beyond the love of wisdom to wisdom itself. Because there is an antinomy of freedom and necessity; and because we can understand this as an antinomy; and because we can

mentally conceive *that* this could be transcended – none of this guarantees in any way that it either is transcended or that we can know how such transcendence is possible. Hegel reconstructs in an immanent fashion the ontological argument for God, and with just as little justification for it. He claims more justification for it, insofar as his god is ego or spirit knowing itself, and not a being external to it. But no more than a theologian can prove the existence of God, can Hegel prove the certainty of a resolution of freedom and necessity. So much the less can he create out of whole cloth a new and so-called deeper kind of knowledge than the human kind of knowledge we actually can possess – a knowledge that is and must be predicated upon our finitude, our persisting self-consciousness. Were there such knowledge, it would indeed be a knowledge that passes all human understanding.

And so it seems that we must somehow fall prey neither to a restrictive essentialist account of human beings nor to a view that as ego we are free to create and re-create the world at will. Can we find a description adequate to the true fullness of human beings without adopting the illusory and self-contradictory concept of a freely creating ego? Martin Heidegger offers a very deep thought about what it means to be human. For Heidegger, a human being is a revealer of being, one who allows beings to come out of their concealment. In this way human beings come out of their concealment from themselves as well. This account is wholly immanent, but at the same time avoids the overreaching of contemporary idealist egoism. After all, though there is a reciprocal un-concealing which occurs, it is not as if human beings have created the concealment of being in the first place, and not as if they somehow *are* the very beings which are brought out of concealment.

All this is fair enough and well said. What is less clear is that this understanding is new. Indeed, it hardly seems like an

advance over the ancient Greek oracle's dictum to "know yourself" or Eckhart's dictum to "go beyond God to go to God." Coming to know ourselves and the external world is a result not of blind forces working behind us, but of discrete human beings who do not and will not rest content with partial, abstracted ideas of what it means to be human. We must continually push forward beyond every limited view, toward the fullness of what is human. And there is no guarantee, indeed there is not even any good reason to suppose that this process will end with a conclusion in which we can rest simply, smugly and self-sufficiently satisfied.

What does such a life look like? What is a life which presses beyond all essentialist views of human beings as tribal members, as souls, as embodied wills, or as minds? What is a life which is open to the fullness of human being, but which understands that such openness is not infinite and complete, but is always somehow rooted in the finitude of a persisting self-awareness? How shall we come truly to know ourselves?

Nature/ The External World

With the external world, we would live in a continual state of wonderment that all that exists does exist. We would be open to what there is, including our own being. This is better captured in German: we would be open to what *es gibt*, that is to say, open to what is *given* to us.

To look upon the world and all within it, including our own being, as "given" is bound to invoke a certain wonder or surprise. It may, depending on the temperament of the observer, also generate responses from pious gratitude to Schopenhauerian disgust – but wonder is the underlying and more or less inevitable response of anyone who has ever contemplated all that is given to him. This sense of wonder is far from the sense of creative mastery of the contemporary ego.

It is far from the idea that the external world is merely given its qualities on loan by the freely creative ego. It is far from the idea that the external world is merely "standing reserve" waiting to be shaped and utilized by the creative ego. It is far from being a "mere pensioner" on human ego.

To the contrary, the sense of wonder suggests the possibility, even the likelihood that what is outside of us can itself offer or bring something to a relationship with a human being. Goethe once described his orientation to the external world in a most revealing manner. He said that he aimed "…to preserve my individual nature according to its peculiarities, and to let external nature influence me according to its qualities." To allow external nature to influence us according to its qualities is of course to presume that external nature *has* qualities. It is to presume that external nature itself can bring something to a relationship with a human being because it exists in such a way that what *es gibt* is not merely material for our manipulation. It is to presume that we are not immanent gods who are free to create the world out of the formless void as we please.

In a letter discussing his *Duino Elegies*, the poet Rainer Maria Rilke says:

> Nature, the things we move about among and use, are provisional and perishable; but, so long as we are here, they are *our* possession and our friendship, sharers in our trouble and gladness, just as they have been the confidants of our ancestors.

Yes, external nature is our possession, but not merely as a plaything of ego. External nature can offer meanings to human beings, as indeed it does all the time. Its meanings are significant to human beings, to be sure – but it does not follow that we put them there at random or that they owe their entire being to us.

We should be clear here. Is not the very idea of "nature" a human creation? Does not the external world of "things" require human beings in order to come out of its concealed potentiality to actuality? Without a doubt, the external world can be recognized (re-cognized) for what it is only by a human (or some other) mind. It is and can be known only by the classifying, schematizing ways in which it is given fixity by human beings or other relatively conscious beings. It is this very fixedness – which we know is subject to change depending upon our human purposes and intentions – which makes possible our practical or our scientific manipulation of the external world. It could not be otherwise, and in this way the emergence of the external world into the light of human understanding depends upon that very human understanding. But is it altogether without warrant to suppose that what is a necessary condition is also a fully sufficient condition for such emergence. This is the extraordinary leap that contemporary egoism makes. Because human beings are necessary to the emergence of the external world of things does not mean that human beings are free to create that emergence in any way we please. Even if it is the glory of the world to emerge into the light of human understanding – to be transformed, in Rilke's word – this emergence is no necessary result of the empty human ego freely creating it as it might be pleased to do so.

To the contrary, we humans and the external world of things emerge together, in a reciprocal way. Without human self-emergence, there would be no visible or known world, to be sure. But we humans are a part of that process of emergence, not some abstract entity which stands wholly outside and beyond the process, much less an entity which *is* the entire process itself. In the ancient Greek sense of *phusis*, the whole world is emergent. But we are a part of the self-emergent world, as our

entire psychosomatic human being is itself shaped in this process of emergence.

To look upon our ideas of "nature" or of "justice" or of the entire thing-comprised external world as requiring human participation is one thing. But to conclude that there is a pure arbitrariness to these worlds is without any basis at all. It is simply to assume away that to which we must always be open if we are to live a genuinely thoughtful life. It is to indulge in what might aptly be called the complete narcissism of the human ego. It is the narcissism of an ego which concludes that it, and it alone, is uniquely different from and superior to all else that exists. Indeed, in its pure form, it concludes that all else that exists is a (misunderstood) version of itself.

In the emergence of human being and the external world, there is a certain kinship between humans and all else there is. It is not a kinship like that described by Fichte, Schelling, or Hegel, who root that kinship in the idea that the external world is ego. For these idealists, the external world, even if in an alien fashion, seems weirdly familiar to ourselves because it is our creation. It is rather more a kinship like that described by Goethe. For Goethe, the world is neither "standing reserve" nor an alienated creation of ourselves. For Goethe, the kinship between us and the external world is founded in a fundamentally and entirely different way, namely, that both we and the external world have been given to ourselves. Just as we did not create the external world, neither did we create ourselves. We have found the whole world, including ourselves, put here and given to us. The fundamental ground upon which the external world is able to contribute its "qualities" to human understanding in this: we share the quality of being with the external world. Specific types of beings may provoke and call for specific types of responses, and it is upon this that all notions of justice are founded. We will say more of

this is due course. But at its broadest, we and the entire world share the quality of being. This is not a sharing we have caused to happen, but a sharing which is given to us. It is a sharing which once seemed quite normal, but which now needs to be raised into consciousness in order not to seem bizarre or unusual. This broad sharing does not necessarily dictate a specific kind of response, but it does call for a general orientation toward what else shares in it. Other beings might well serve as mere objects for our use. But they can also be more than that. They possess being as we do, and from this a certain wonder, a certain respect, and a certain openness to hear what they are "saying" is fully appropriate.

By virtue of being in being, we share a very deep quality that roots us fully at home in the world. This is not an aesthetic orientation toward the world. An aesthetic attitude toward the world does not provoke desire or will; it gazes upon the world from the outside, as it were, with a suppressed will. It is as if that old bachelor Kant, who defined aesthetics as that which does not provoke desire, could gaze upon the beauty of a woman, but seek no further relationship with her. The aesthetic attitude remains an abstracted, double-mediated approach to the external world – an approach which is the mirror image of the world as standing reserve. It is a relationship to the external world rooted in the narcissistic, alienated understanding of nature and the external world as that which differs from human ego. In short, an aesthetic orientation toward the external world is not founded in the shared kinship of being.

To live based upon the shared relation of being with all else that exists is a life in the world, not a life in which our being is suppressed to the status of a passive observer. It is a life in which our own being emerges concomitantly with the emergence of the external world out of its formlessness. We cannot say in advance – and we cannot perhaps ever say fully –

what is given to us and what we give to the external world as we aim to learn the full extent of our human latitude. But the cardinal point is that we should live with an openness to the idea that both what is outside ourselves, as well as our very being itself, are somehow given to us, and not merely made up by ourselves. Goethe speaks to this attitude in his *Maxims and Reflections* (#1140) when he says:

> It is a pleasant occupation to inquire into nature and into one's own self at the same time; not to force either nature or one's own spirit, but to bring both into a balanced relationship by a gentle reciprocal influence.

On Life With Others

As human beings, we give meaning – and even bring into clarity the being of being – to the rest of the world. In doing this we both cooperate with and struggle with other human beings. We inherit some meanings, we modify others, and we pass along still others – invariably in a social context in which we interact with other human beings. We seek, in and through all of our human relationships, to understand what is the being of what there is. This effort – whether it is found in a mother's injunctions to her children to behave, a teacher's instructions, a spouse's expectations, or in the guidelines of any other social interaction or institution – is always in search of finding out how things are. This discovery is motivated by, and is at once the simultaneous discovery of how we are to comport ourselves. The most comprehensive of these institutions is found in political life. Here what is implicit in all other social institutions becomes explicit: here we seek as human beings to say directly, overtly and intentionally what is and what is not appropriate to we humans – that is, to seek to discover what is justice.

The question of how humans think of themselves and the

question of justice: are these questions really commensurate? After all, we inhabit a modern world in which, as David Hume wrote in his *Treatise of Human Nature* (III, I, I), we cannot derive an "ought" from an 'is.' Contemporary philosophers argue along with Hume that no choice or action can be rightly inferred from any description of what is a human being; no description of a human being can or does entail any obligation as to how one *should* act. But we act all the time as if it does. We are forever calling upon one another to "grow up," to "act your age," to "behave like a lady," to "be a man," or to "use your head." We are forever referring to one another as "sick," or "impaired," or "inhuman," or otherwise failing to measure up to some standard of what is a human being. Can these everyday understandings really be so wrong?

Of course they can. It is quite possible that our everyday understandings could be wrong, or at least misleading and inadequately thought through. But it is the very purpose of our everyday understandings to embed a structure of "ought" into every single description of what "is." Uttering so seemingly neutral a description as "this table is broken" holds a wealth of "ought" within it. Implicit in the idea of brokenness is a concept of a table – what is intended by the word "table" – as an object to eat upon, to sit at, or to rest things upon. And it carries the not at all unwarranted inference that it might be more or less useful (that is, perhaps "broken" or perhaps solid and stable) for meeting its ends, for achieving the being of a table. Our everyday world operates in and through a web of seemingly neutral, fact-like statements that contain within them an entire universe of oughts. Implicit within them is a world of intention, of teleology, and of the better or worse fulfillment of being and capability.

The search for a pure, simple language that conveys no such implications – such as formal logic or mathematics – can

succeed as a human enterprise. But what is the warrant to ascribe to that language a higher standing than everyday language, language whose very purpose is to convey such inferences and intentions? Moreover, when one seeks to employ such a language as logic or mathematics, when one plays these games, there is a clear implication that, whatever else, one must play by the rules (the oughts) of the game, because the rules are not only intrinsic to the game, they *are* the game.

If we root the idea of justice in the search for what is the proper description of a human being, there is another advantage: we do not have to make up an imaginary world of "moral sentiments" that exists side by side with the fact-based world of science. We need not try to root practices that might be described as "altruistic" in outlandish theories about how such behavior is truly operating in a hidden way to ensure the survival of organisms or even of the genes within those organisms. These fashionable theories simply move the idea of intention or meaning out of its understandable human context and impute it to some larger, hidden force that lies beyond our choices and actions.

It is characteristic of contemporary thought to follow Hume and to draw a sharp distinction between what or how things are and what they mean. This distinction was given its contemporary form in what is called the difference between "facts" and "values." No one gives better expression to this than the pragmatist William James, who takes over the fact-value distinction wholly from its neo-Kantian authors. James asserts in his *Varieties of Religious Experience* that there are two radically different kinds of intellectual "judgment," the judgment of what a thing is and of what it means. James says:

> Neither judgment can be deduced immediately
> from the other. They proceed from diverse

> intellectual preoccupations, and the mind combines them only by making them first separately, and then adding them together.

Here is to be found one of the cardinal tenets of contemporary egoism. Ego creates a world of science (of how things "are," and so forth) and a world of human meanings and choices. The world of science produces facts or information useful to ego's intentions, but it is not related to these meanings or intentions in any but an instrumental way. But this completely inverts and misunderstands facts and meanings. Were one to be gratuitously negative, one might say that such a profoundly mistaken conclusion could arise only in the ivory tower study of an academic. For surely in the world of day-to-day activity – from a mother and a child to the struggles of people to find justice in a political order – the reality is everywhere exactly the opposite. What one calls something, how one conceives of it and describes it, is everywhere and always pointing toward how one should orient oneself toward it (that is, its meaning). How one thinks of the nature or origin of anything always points in the first instance to some conclusion about it – that is, what is its importance, its significance, its meaning.

James offers an example of how fact/origin is to be distinguished from value/meaning. He says that the human impulse toward deep religiosity originates in neurotic behavior. But for all of that, he says that this does not mean that religiosity is thereby discredited. Its value is to be judged by its fruits, not its origins. But what is the basis for judging an origin to be "neurotic?" It is that this example of behavior displays similarities to other cases of behavior, and we thereby class them together. But this is surely too easy. For how do we come to see these behaviors as "neurotic" in the first place, unless it is against some pre-assumed template of what is "normal?" It is

not necessary to reject James' pragmatic view that outcomes are to be judged by their "fruitfulness" in order to reject his view that the meaning of outcomes is simply and arbitrarily "added to" some readily agreed-upon base of facts.

It is the character of human beings to learn from one another and to contend with one another in the search to understand what objects and institutions and practices are and thus how we should orient ourselves toward them. Consider several examples from contemporary political debates. The issue of abortion is framed by competing understandings. Is abortion a "choice" or is it the murder of an unborn child? This debate does not rest upon an agreed set of factual understandings of what is abortion, which then proceeds to draw divergent conclusions or meanings. To the contrary, there is no agreement on the description of the event itself, of what abortion is. Both contending parties aim to win the argument by securing agreement with their own description of what abortion *is*. Now it could be said that there is perhaps some level of agreement, that is, that abortion is the termination of the life of a fetus. After all, both sides are contending over something they mutually understand to be at issue. But this agreement only removes the problem a degree away. For what is a fetus? If a fetus is a living human being, then is there any more reason to allow the "choice" to end its life than to end the life of any other innocent human being? To win the debate over how to describe abortion is to go a long way toward knowing its meaning as a human practice.

We also struggle today over the issue of "terrorism." How are the acts which we in the modern West describe as terrorism to be understood? To a fervent advocate of radical Islam, the acts which we label as terrorism are in fact the commands of a god; they are acts which will be rewarded, not punished, in a future life. These acts are not described as terrorism, which we

might define as the taking of innocent life in order to instill fear for political ends – but as the taking of guilty life, and thus as fully just and appropriate. Can this difference be reconciled? Perhaps, to a degree. But the point is that how we are to orient ourselves toward these actions does not derive from different "moral sentiments," but from the very description and understanding of what these acts are. These differences most assuredly do not arise from the calm ground of a settled fact-value distinction, where we all agree on the facts but draw different value-laden conclusions from them. To the contrary, the acts themselves are understood and described in fundamentally different ways, ways that point directly toward how they should be evaluated.

These examples could be replicated over and over at every level of human interaction, from mothers and children to the political order. It is the very character of human relationships that they seek to define the facts from which meaning and orientation is drawn. The facts and values begin together, as it were, and in practical life usually persist together until one understanding of the "facts" becomes more or less generally accepted. Contrary to James, the mind does not begin with a prefabricated disjunction of facts and value judgments, which disjunction can be overcome only by "adding" them together. The mind customarily begins in the practical unity of facts and values, and it is only by virtue of patient, careful, rigorous and all-too-rare thinking that the mind can, at least to some degree, subject this unity to questions that might cause one to think differently about it. This is never easy, and surely not as natural as James suggests.

Because our knowing and our interpretation of meaning set out together, we would rightly suppose that knowing is not a dispassionate, instrumental enterprise. To the contrary, it is rooted fully in the effort to orient ourselves in the world. The

superficial contemporary reading of ancient Greek philosophy stereotypes that philosophy as a kind of parallel thought-world alongside the world of passion, a world which presumes to give direction to our passions from the outside, as it were. This is plain wrong, both as a doctrine and as an interpretation of ancient philosophy which is everywhere founded in the unified human origin of thought and passion, of thought as a kind of motion, a special case of being en-souled. This misreading of ancient philosophy is not simply benign, because it is intended to set off and to defend the modern, opposite conclusion, namely, that passion (the choices of ego) is the master of human life and that thinking is merely its servant. But it is every bit as misguided to set reason and passion apart and to elevate the passions as would be the opposite approach. The so-called primacy of "moral intuitions" needlessly and unjustifiably depreciates thinking, whereas in fact it is by way of our very thinking and knowing that we express our so-called moral intuitions.

It is the character of human life to struggle continually in all of our relationships to express and to adjust our ideas of justice – that is, *how we are to understand what there is and who we are.* This process takes place within all of our social institutions from the relation of a mother and child to the complexities of a political order. There is no such thing as a personal ethics, apart from the social context and interactions through which our views have emerged. While we can certainly act on the basis of our own thoughts, and while these thoughts might be to some degree unique, it is not as if these thoughts have sprung wholly out of a mysteriously a-social potentiality-bearing ego. To the contrary, they have emerged as humans aim to clarify their sense of what it means to be human from interactions with other human beings. Even the hermit, who may take advantage of pure

solitude to purify his thoughts, works with the raw material provided by prior social interactions.

To live well, then, is to understand and to accept ourselves as members of our social context and not as a purely potentiality-bearing ego. Our social context does not exhaust the fullness of our being – but neither is it to be understood as an arbitrary limitation on our being, much less as a hindrance to realizing our humanity. To the contrary, the various social relationships of our life are a genuine and intrinsically important part of what it means to be a human being. This means: if you are a father, act like a father. If you are a husband, act like a husband. If you are a citizen of America, act like one. These are not roles – they are each a genuine portion of your human being. These features of your being are not to be cast off at will. Act according to the manifold fullness of the human being which you are. Do not do so because there is a reward which will maximize your potential to be or to do something else. What, after all, would be the point of being able to be something else? Act in all the ways that you are rooted in your social/political world because you are so rooted. These are a part of your being; they are your being. They are not roles or costumes which you can put on and take off at will. Your children, your spouse, your fellow citizens are who they are. This *is* your life.

Seeking justice, or living a life which is appropriate to a human being, cannot and should not become fixed on only one aspect of our manifold human being. Being a husband or a father to the exclusion of all else will result in diminishing, or even missing, other portions of our being. Being a full-time practitioner of an economic profession will result in excluding other portions of our being. Being a citizen to the exclusion of all else will result in slighting other qualities which we genuinely are. To be sure, there is great force or power to be

gained in elevating or accentuating a single quality of our multifold being at the expense of all others. To understand ourselves, to define ourselves entirely by our economic profession, as a spouse, as a parent, as a loyal citizen, or as a servant of one's god can result in powerful and awe-inspiring actions; but we are all that we are, and we cannot slough off or ignore or deny the many very real qualities of our being without denying significant aspects of all that we are, that is, of doing justice to our entire human being. It is tempting to allow some relationship, or set of relationships, to define ourselves to the exclusion of all else that we truly are. It is often the case that living such a life produces surprising and unpleasant consequences when the suppressed aspects of one's being come to light and express themselves. But whether or not such a crisis occurs, a life which denies the fullness of our being is a life which is not fully human, that is, it is a life of less than full justice toward ourselves.

If it is a mistake to exclude some aspects of our being to serve another, so much less sense does it make to aim to strip away *every* distinguishing character of our being in order to know ourselves, to find justice. The kind of justice that requires a veil of ignorance which hides each and every unique social characteristic of our human being is a perfect "justice" for a world of egos. It is an attempt to found a notion of justice on the pure power to choose without regard to our entire being, but only with regard to the sheer capacity to choose. But we are not like this, and this thought experiment offers no guidance to actual human beings. The unreal choices made behind a veil of ignorance could never in principle offer either knowledge or guidance about how to live. In short, there is no justice to be found down the course of ignorance, whether it is happenstance ignorance or, so much the less, willful ignorance.

The manifold character of human being surely suggests

some very real limitations on justice. We are complex beings with many qualities and knowing how to express and to balance them is a difficult task. Our notions of justice can and will guide our choices. But for the complex beings which we are, perfect justice is little likely to uniform each and every specific choice we confront. It is implausible that knowledge of who we are in all our complexity will dictate clear-cut guidance for each of life's daily and often minor dilemmas. This is the practical advantage of codes of revealed religion: they offer clear-cut guidance to supplement what self-knowledge we actually can and do possess. Judging the justice of a man upon one or another specific choice, however, is akin to judging an author based upon one word or one phrase in his text. What justice we can find will be found at the level of an entire human life, lived in its complex and balanced fullness.

The elevation of a specific human quality to the essence of human life has at least one virtue. Finding the essence of human being in our membership in a tribe or nation, for example, roots human beings in our time and place, as members of a given set of social/political relationships. This is a real and vital part of what it means to be a human being – it speaks to a portion of what *is* about one's life, and therefore expresses some degree of justice. But it is clearly not sufficient, because it locates our essence in our tribal membership, which in turn does not do justice to other aspects of our human being. It is in this way partially unjust.

But this partial injustice cannot be transcended by leaping over, or out of, our given world. We may be able to transcend that world, but we can do so only by understanding both its limitations and its contributions. We must accept all that we are in order to come to know ourselves better. In this way we understand that even if we know that we are not merely a member of the tribe, but something more as well, we still are, for

all of that, a member of the tribe. The proper response to this reality is not to conclude that the web of social, tribal and political relations which comprise so large a portion of our life are to be viewed negatively, as restraints upon our presumed true self. To the contrary, they have helped to make us all that we are, and they continue to do so. The proper response is to understand that each and every one of these institutional and personal relationships has helped to make us what we are. We have not made ourselves, over and against our social and political lives. These institutions have not inhibited our self-knowledge, but are the inevitable, if partial, basis upon which our self-knowledge can and does arise. The proper response is not to disparage our institutions as chains on the free exercise of our egos to become all they can be – but one of gratitude for making possible our limited chance to know ourselves. It is not, as Maslow says, that we must "free" ourselves of other people in order to become fully ourselves. We rather should express gratitude to others for their inescapable role is helping us achieve our limited chance to know ourselves better. Knowing that we are not only members of a tribe is necessary to live a fully human life. But knowing that we are and always will be rooted in the social/political relationships that comprise our life is also necessary. In expressing gratitude for these social institutions, in seeking to orient them more fully to justice, and in passing them along to those who come after us – this is a fuller, and hence more just, knowing of our human being.

The Gods

What are we to make of the gods and the claims which have been advanced so forcefully on their behalf? We should seek from this standpoint: there may be a god or gods and a fully human life requires us to seek to know their being and their will. Justice requires us to orient ourselves to what there *is*, including

the possibility of the gods. We should never simply rationalize our own current desires, whatever they may happen to be. Reason is not and never ought to be the slave of the passions. And that is true for our orientation to the gods as well. This does not mean we should overlook our current desires, much less aim to suppress or obliterate them. Our desires must be accepted and understood for what they are. Obliterating our desires – or at least pretending to – is no more fruitful than imagining ourselves to be freely floating ego without any roots in a social/political order in time and space. But we ought never to rest content with our own desires as they are at any given moment, knowing full well that they can, and indeed perhaps should, change as we learn more of our human being.

This is to say that we must always be open to the idea that there is an order or a structure or a force in the universe that is not evident at the current moment. This might look more or less like an abstract force, more or less like a personal god; but in no event does it make sense to be dogmatic about what we do not currently know. This course is the way to be open to what *es gibt* in the fullest human way. It is to entertain the premise that ultimately there is more in the world than ego. It is to orient ourselves as if there is, or at least could be, a being or a force in the universe to which we can and should re-spond. It is to suppose that ego is not the measure of all things, for as we have seen, such an ego would itself lack the framework by which to measure anything at all.

As human beings, perhaps it is finally not possible to comprehend a world force or spirit or god in any way other than based upon analogy to human willing and the human capacity to act. This may constitute a bound to our understanding. But whether it is a bound or not, it is surely a strong hint to avoid any and all signs of dogmatism about the gods. The gods must be thought of in such a way that we

remain open to the idea that our human comprehension may be inadequate to conceive of or to imagine them.

It is everywhere the temptation to do just the opposite. In a letter to a correspondent, Spinoza said wittily, but with sharp insight:

> I believe that a triangle, if it could speak, would likewise say that God is eminently triangular, and a circle that God's nature is eminently circular. In this way each would ascribe to God its own attributes, assuming itself to be like God and regarding all else as ill-formed.

And so it is; we find that the doctrines of revealed religion often *are* little more than broad rationalizations for human preferences or human hopes, as they express themselves in one or another time and place, in one or another social/political order. The commands of revealed religion reflect human purposes, as do the very ways in which the gods who issue these commands are imagined to be. In this sense, many of the gods which human beings have worshipped have been disguised versions of their own preferences and hopes. The criticisms of Hegel, Feuerbach and the other authors of contemporary egoism are, in this sense, fair enough. Most gods seem familiar to us and their commands are understandable to us because we *have* created them and their ostensible commands. A god of the universe who advises tribal members which food to eat on which day might reasonably be supposed to reflect the customs of the tribe, or the intentions of a tribal lawgiver. The revelations of such gods themselves change their accent over time as the peoples who worship them change. To suppose these gods are adjusting their revelations over time to comport with or to "reach" people in changed circumstances is a latter day occasionalism which, like its predecessor, cannot be disproved

in a convincing way – but which there is neither any good reason to suppose to be true.

As Spinoza suggests, it may well be the human tendency to conceive of our gods in human terms. This is a normal phenomenon, and it is not so much that we cannot move beyond it, as that it is a customary human starting place. Just as the so-called "facts" of our social life reflect at once our intentions and preferences and hopes, so do our ideas about the gods as well. For this reason, we should be wary when we encounter full-blown instructions from the gods which address each and every aspect of human practice. So much the more so when the gods are identified with a particular people, or tongue, or nation – be it the people of Israel, the language of Arabic, or the providential status of the United States.

This kind of inverted (or alienated) worship of our own or our own group's preferences is not the core of a fully human openness to the gods. A genuine openness to the gods is at once openness to the idea that there is more in the universe than ego. The supposition that ego is the standard for everything is a supposition in need of a very high standard of evidence, and indeed much higher than has ever yet been offered. To fail to be open to the gods is akin to a color-blind person being dogmatic about colors. "Show me the evidence" for the gods is a decent demand; but we must not be too dogmatic about what such evidence might look like, or about what form in which it arrives. We should remain open to the idea that there are gods or beings or forces which we have not created, and to which it would be appropriate to respond. Now we may or may not discover these gods or these forces, and it is even less likely that highly detailed commands about how to live will be forthcoming. But it is through this very openness that we come best to understand what is genuinely possible for human beings to know, both about the universe and about ourselves.

We would be well-advised to look beyond the elaborate instructions of the "will of the gods" to find a deeper, less humanly contrived form of self-worship. This is well spoken by Meister Eckhart in "On Riddance." There he says that the hardest thing for humans to do is to give up God – to go to God. We must go beyond our prejudices about the gods to be open to the possibility of the gods.

We cannot live a fully human life by worshipping our own prejudices or desires, whether they are for material, sensual goods or for the gods. So much less sense is there to live by predicating the conduct of our life upon an elaborate account of the afterlife. We may well be limited in our capability to conceive the qualities of the gods. But at least behind these qualities lies an abstract concept of god or the gods, somehow imagined on an analogy to force or power or mover. Of the afterlife, there is no warrant to say even this. The idea of an afterlife is rooted neither in the conceptual necessity to account for what there *is*, nor in the necessity to remind us of our human finitude. An afterlife might or might not exist; but it is in no way necessary to imagine such a condition in order to live in the world we are in. Nor is it a necessary corrective to the idea that ego has created all there is. To the contrary, the idea of an afterlife seems a pure flight of speculative fancy, which looks suspiciously more like the creation of ego than a counterpose to it.

If there is no conceptual necessity for the idea of an afterlife, there is even less that could properly be predicated about it. No less a figure than Augustine says so. The afterlife is a supposed second creation of the gods, in tandem with the first, but lacking any and all sensible characteristics and thus any and all ways to be known. Were it possible to form clear images of an afterlife based upon human experience, perhaps the many and bizarre accounts of it might be more easily

reconcilable. It is not that the prospect of an afterlife is necessarily unwelcome;[*] it is that the notion that this life can be described in any meaningful way is literally non-sensical. There has never been, nor will there ever be, a more complete and true statement about the afterlife than that attributed in Plato's *Apology* to Socrates:

> But now the time has come to go away. I go to
> die and you to live; but which of us goes to the
> better lot, is known to none but God.

To orient our life in this world that we *do* have according to the prospect of reward and punishment in a speculative afterlife is unwarranted and even a bit perverse. It is somewhat akin to worshipping a purely abstracting ego which is alleged to lie "behind" all human experiences. It is to make the human creation of ego the arbiter of our choices. It is to put what is unreal in place of what is real. This is not to set too high a standard for human beings; it is to set the wrong standard altogether. It is slavish and ignoble to worship the gods because we might be rewarded (or at least not punished) in an imagined afterlife. Here God is sought not because he might exist, but only for narrow self-advantage. Down this course lies an overly fearful view of death; down this course lies injustice, that is, an unwillingness to seek what is simply because it is.

Far better to live a life predicated upon the world in which we find ourselves. Rilke says in the *Duino Elegies*:

> ...because being here amounts to so much,
> because all this Here and Now, so fleeting,
> seems to require us and strangely concerns us,
> Us the most fleeting of all. Just once, every-

---

[*] Goethe says in his *Conversations with Eckermann*: "I should be well pleased if, after the close of this life, we were blessed with another, only I hope I should hereafter meet none of those who had believed in it here."

> thing, only for once. Once and no more. And
> we, too, once. And never again. But this having
> been once, though only once, having been once
> on earth – it cannot be revoked.

Far better the fullness of being in this life than to sacrifice it for imaginary self-preservation. Far better, too, a sense of our own finitude that supposes that the world will go on without us, that it is not a creation of ego which will perish along with our own life.

It is enough to be open to the gods because one seeks what there is (what *es gibt*). Such a life is not lived in order to achieve the uncertain certainties of specific knowledge of god's will. Here, however, we encounter the dilemma of every notion of a fully transcendent god. Such a god is so far from human beings that nothing can be known about him. And as Cardinal Newman says in *The Idea of a University*:

> I do not see much difference between avowing
> that there is no God, and implying that nothing
> definite can be known for certain about Him.

It is not that the gods necessarily must be conceived as fully transcendent; they could partake of immanence and wish to make themselves known to human beings. Indeed, such gods as may exist could make themselves known to human beings only in the way(s) in which humans can know. It is impossible to disprove the notion of a god so transcendent that he would be unavailable to human comprehension. Indeed, one could not disprove in this sense the idea of a god so transcendent that, were it his will, he would have human beings practice idolatry. Nothing would oblige such a god to reveal the truth to human beings. But such a god is a pure creation of fancy, as we could know of the gods only in the way(s) in which it is possible for us to know.

In seeking what *there is*, we orient ourselves profoundly against the striving of an imaginary ego which is supposed to have created the entire world. In short, we must open out our being beyond the rationalization of our own prejudices and preferences about what we call god – in order to be open to god. In this way, we aim to uncover what there is, and how to orient ourselves toward it. This is the standpoint of a human being who rejects the mythology of the self-creating ego. This is at once the way to knowledge of ourselves. It is at once a knowing of ourselves, that is, of justice.

Interior Life

How are we to think of ourselves? We will seek to under-stand our being as we really are – the we that is characterized by all that we are, not the being which is somehow alleged to live and to act behind or beneath all that we are. We are *all* that we are, including our body, our time and place, and all of the social relations that make up our being. We are all that we are, including the manifold ways in which outside powers or forces act upon us. This being that we are cannot be found by looking "inside" to find a pure ego unsullied by contact with the external world. To the contrary, in the first instance it is through the external world that we orient oneselves. Goethe expresses this when he says that throughout his life he aimed:

> to regard the external with love; and to allow all
> beings from man downwards...to act upon me,
> each after its own kind.

To allow other beings to act upon us – this is to be a being which *can* be acted upon. After all, no external being can act upon the ego; its very being excludes such a possibility in favor of the ego shaping the external world. The ego is a myth-ological private "place" which cannot be acted upon, which

cannot be shaken, and which is pure freedom itself. If the pure freedom of ego were shaped by what is outside, it would no longer be free.

Freely choosing ego finds in the external world only raw materials upon which to exercise its creative freedom. It finds nothing beyond itself that possesses its own character, and therefore the ability to shape it in any way. To allow the external world to act upon us is not only to be able to be acted upon; it is also to look upon the external world as having the capability to act upon us. More, it is supposing that the external world is *worthy* of acting upon us. Again Goethe speaks to this most eloquently. In rejecting the ego philosophy of his contemporaries – and their definition of freedom – Goethe says in his *Conversations with Eckermann*:

> Freedom consists not in refusing to recognize anything above us, but in respecting something which is above us; for, by respecting it, we raise ourselves to it, and by our very acknowledgment make manifest that we bear within ourselves what is higher, and we are worthy to be on a level with it.

There is much about human beings to be pondered. But in doing so, the task is not to turn away from all that we are, and from the entire world of our existence, to find within ourselves a pure core being, or ego. This would be to let go of all that is, and of all we are, in order to seek what we actually are not. It would be to substitute the genuine freedom which Goethe describes to grow beyond our current being, with an elusive freedom which turns out to be only the tyranny of momentary desires. It would be to seek freedom in the whims of passing desire rather than in recognition of what is. It would be to act unwittingly and to call the result "freedom."

It is not really possible to start all over again. We may find

in what is external a new and higher model for life, and we may aim to emulate that model. This is all to the good – but it is not as if this process is an internal act of ego, which somehow manages to break free of all external restraints. Even if we are "born anew," we are born into the same time, place, body, family, and nationality that characterized us before. No matter how far and how quickly emulating a new model may take us, we remain in some degree the creature that we are and have been. This reality neither can nor should be sloughed off. To use William James' terms—but to invert his conclusion—the "I" is not freely creating a "me" as it goes about appropriating and assembling experiences. In a very real way, the "me" is continually shaping the "I." It is shaping the horizon within which an "I" exists. This horizon is not narrowly circumscribed by anything so singular as the means of production, or any other so-called determinant of "false consciousness." This horizon can and does move; it moves as the "me" shapes the "I" – which is merely a name for me right now – which in turn shapes the "me" that will be.

We cannot find our uniqueness by looking inside ourselves. Our uniqueness derives not from within, but from the very web of relations with the external world which comprises us and our being. We are unique because of this only-once, this time and place we occupy, this body which shapes us, this place we hold within our families, and this sociopolitical world which encompasses us. Our uniqueness comes from how we are fitted into our context in the external world. There is this only-once of Jeff Bergner not because of some mysterious quality lying behind and within me, but because of the complex set of relationships with the external world that comprises who I am.

We come then to an interesting and ironic conclusion. Our uniqueness does not derive from our separateness, but from the web of our relationships with the external world, with the gods,

and with other human beings. But at the same time we *know* that we are unique, we understand that we are uniquely one existing being – and we therefore know that there are other (uniquely) existing beings as well. When we think about this, we understand that our uniqueness lies precisely in our discreteness, our finitude, and that it is somehow possible to be otherwise than we are. We may be American and not French, for example – but we know there is a French nation and we know, to some degree at least, what it means to be French. This knowledge does not and cannot make us French, in the way of those who are born and raised French. But this knowledge does permit us, if we should for some reason choose to emulate this model, to try to become more French. So, too, with the entire web of relationships that makes us unique. In the very act of knowing, we transcend our finitude and our uniqueness. We do not thereby actually become native-born French—much less have we created the French—but we can somehow know both our uniqueness and more than our uniqueness.

In thinking about our uniqueness and what defines this uniqueness, we somehow transcend this uniqueness. We somehow are not entirely "filled up by" or sated by our uniqueness. It is in thinking that we partially overcome our uniqueness. Thinking seems to be the most selfish possible activity; it requires no one else to be present and can occur in virtually any social or natural context. It is in thinking that we find a world that operates most independently from the constraints of time, place, family, finances, nationality, and even bodily imprisonment. But ironically, thinking is how we most successfully transcend our limits. Thinking is a kind of catharsis by which we transcend – to the degree we are able – the limitations and unique fixedness of our time and place. Thinking is the most selfish activity, which ironically takes us beyond our limits, to become less selfish. It is for this reason that Meister Eckhart

said: "The truth is that the more ourselves we are, the less ego is in us."

In thinking we give expression to a desire to escape our bounds of space and time, and in so doing we also give expression to a very real portion of our human being. It is not enough to be only a member of a tribe and to know or define ourselves completely through the network of the tribe. Doing so omits a very significant quality of what it means to live a fully human life. We are always somehow more than the totality of our web of relationships. Aiming to sublimate that quality of "moreness" in our relationship to nature, to a tribe, or to the gods fails to give expression to this portion of our being. Obedience is at best a partial virtue, and one which fails to exercise the distinctively human character of being in, but at once beyond, our environment. It is not that we could not live a relatively happy life as an obedient member of a tribe or another political community, finding our fulfillment in that set of relationships; it is that this is inevitably less than a fully human life.

Nor is it possible to find our "essence" in sloughing off all our particularities—to find our "essence," for example, in a disembodied mind. We can partially transcend our bodies in the act of thinking, but we cannot divorce ourselves from them. Elevating mind, or that exercise of soul that ancients called mind, does not in fact detach us from our body. Nor does it do justice to the way in which the qualities of our bodies in-form our thinking. Christian church doctrine is in this way correct, that to be human is inevitably to be a psychosomatic unity, or what the encyclical "Gaudium et Spes" calls "*corpere et anima unus*." Christian doctrine aims to offer transcendence of the here and now by imagining a permanent, ongoing psychosomatic unity in another world. This notion, however, does not really clarify the question of what it means to live in a fully human